THE JOURNEY BEGINS

LESSONS LEARNED IN THE WILDERNESS
(BOOK 1)

KENNETH A. WINTER

WildernessLessons

JOIN MY READERS' GROUP FOR UPDATES AND FUTURE RELEASES

i am mindful that i am simply a "beggar" who desires to share with other "beggars" where he found bread as we all make this journey together.

Please join my Readers' Group so i can send you a free book, as well as updates and information about future releases in the series.

See the back of the book for details on how to sign up.

* * *

The Journey Begins

Book #1 in the **Lessons Learned In The Wilderness** series.

Published by:

Kenneth A. Winter

WildernessLessons

Richmond, Virginia

United States of America

kenwinter.org / wildernesslessons.com

Cover Design: Melanie Fisher-Wellman

ISBN 978-1-7240714-5-3 (soft cover)

ISBN 978-0-9755897-0-0 (ebook)

Library of Congress Control Number: 2004094507

CONTENTS

DEDICATION

* * *

For my life partner, LaVonne, and our children, Justin and Lorél, as we journey by faith together though this wilderness. And for our dear family – those by birth, as well as those by rebirth – who have been a constant encouragement along the way. But most of all, for the honor and glory of the Lord God Jehovah, who leads us all the way.

* * *

PREFACE

* * *

The God of Abraham, Isaac and Jacob called unto Himself a people - a people through whom the whole world would be blessed – and He led this people on a journey through the wilderness. He promised them that He would watch over them, He would go before them and lead them, He would go behind them and protect them; He promised that He would receive great glory through their journey. And He promised that the journey would end in a land of milk and honey – His Land of Promise. And along the way, God would teach them Who He is so that they might know Him, know Him more and know Him more intimately. The journey was more than just the path to His promise; the journey was a part of God's promise. God was using the journey to prepare His people for all that He was preparing for them in the Land of Promise – that they might experience His Person, witness His power and understand His purpose. They would see Him use this journey for their good and His glory.

God continues to desire to bless the world through His people. If we name the Name of Jesus, we are His children. God has called His children to be on mission with Him to make a global impact. As a part of His mission,

God often leads us on a journey through the wilderness - that place where He prepares us, and that platform that He uses to declare His glory in and through our lives to a watching world. There are lessons that you can only learn in the wilderness. He will use this time to enable you to experience His Person, witness His power and better understand His purpose. Yes, His Land of Promise is on the other side, but don't miss what He has for you in the journey. God has given us the account of the Israelites' journey through the wilderness that we might heed those *"Lessons Learned In The Wilderness"*. May God use the lessons to encourage you, to refresh you and to challenge you in the journey He is leading you in today - as He prepares you to be His ambassador through whom He will make a global impact.

And Jesus said: *"Therefore, go and make disciples of all the nations, baptizing them in the name of the Father and the Son and the Holy Spirit. Teach these new disciples to obey all the commands I have given you. And be sure of this: I am with you always, even to the end of the age."* (Matt 28:19-20)

* * *

A WORD OF EXPLANATION

* * *

You will notice that whenever i use the pronoun "I" referring to myself, i have chosen to use a lowercase "i". It is not a typographical error. i know that is contrary to proper English grammar and accepted editorial style guides. i drive editors (and "spell check") crazy by doing this. But years ago the LORD convicted me – personally – that in all things i must decrease and He must increase. And as a way of continuing personal reminder, from that day forward, i have chosen to use a lower case "i" whenever referring to myself. Because of the same conviction, i use a capital letter for any pronoun referring to God. The style guide for the New Living Translation (NLT) does not share that conviction. However, you will see that i have intentionally made that slight revision and capitalized any pronoun referring to God in my quotations of Scripture from the NLT. If i have violated any style guides as a result, please accept my apology, but i must honor this conviction.

Lastly, regarding this matter – this is a personal conviction – and i share it only so that you will understand why i have chosen to deviate from normal editorial practice. i am in no way suggesting or endeavoring to have anyone else subscribe to my conviction. Thanks for your understanding.

* * *

CHAPTER SCRIPTURE LISTING

* * *

1

A CONFIDENT CRY

Then the children of Israel groaned because of the bondage, and they cried out;
and their cry came up to God because of the bondage. So God heard their
groaning, and God remembered His covenant with Abraham, with Isaac, and with
Jacob. And God looked upon the children of Israel, and God acknowledged them.
Exodus 2:23b-25 (NKJ)

* * *

God was preparing to go global with the announcement of His glory to the entire world – and He had chosen a people through whom He was going to accomplish His purpose. But even though they were His chosen people, they found themselves in bondage to Pharaoh. And they groaned under the weight of their oppression – they groaned to the point that they could no longer endure. Then, they turned to the One who could deliver them from their bondage.

The people cried out to God. Their deliverance began with the people calling upon God. Deliverance will always begin with our recognition that the solution to the problem is beyond ourselves and dependent upon God – that we are powerless in and of ourselves. Repeatedly throughout Scripture, God tells us to call upon Him – that we must come to the end of ourselves and call out to Him. The first step of deliverance is admitting we have a problem and we cannot fix it ourselves – and only God can.

God heard their cries. God has promised us that if we seek Him, we will find Him. Just like the mother's ear is attuned to the whimper or the cry of her child, even more so is the ear of our Heavenly Father. And there is nowhere we can go that He cannot hear us, if we will call out to Him.

God remembered His promise. The God of Abraham, Isaac and Jacob had made a covenant that through this people all the families of the earth would be blessed – that He had chosen them to be His people through whom He would accomplish His purpose for His glory. And our God has made that promise to His adopted children – those who name the name of Christ – that we have been grafted into the Vine with all the rights and privileges of a joint heir – and He has chosen us to be His children through whom He accomplishes His purpose for His glory. He has promised that He will never leave us or forsake us; He has promised that what He begins He completes, and He has sealed His promise through the indwelling presence of His Holy Spirit.

God looked upon His people. His eyes looked upon them with compassion and with purpose. *The eyes of the LORD search the whole earth in order to strengthen those whose hearts are fully committed to Him* (2 Chronicles 16:9). He has fixed His children in His gaze – nothing in our path escapes His attention – and He desires to marshal every resource at His disposal to strengthen them and equip them for His purpose.

God acknowledged them as His children. It was one thing for the people to acknowledge Him as God; but in His acknowledging them as His children, He is acknowledging His love for them and His commitment to them. Yes, He is their Creator; but He declares ownership when He acknowledges them as His creation – and He declares that they are a part of His purpose.

As John wrote in his first epistle, *"This is the confidence which we have before Him, that, if we ask anything according to His will, He hears us. And if we know that He hears us in whatever we ask, we know that we have the requests which we have asked from Him."* God revealed this pattern to the children of Israel when they stopped groaning to themselves under their bondage, and cried out to the One who could make a difference. We, too, can and will experience our deliverance, if we will cease groaning to ourselves, and will turn from ourselves and call out to Him. We can then call unto Him with that same confidence – a confidence that He has assured through His Word, He has enabled through His Son, and He has sealed through His Holy Spirit.

* * *

2

AN INVITATION TO GO

One day Moses was tending the flock of his father-in-law, Jethro, the priest of Midian, and he went deep into the wilderness near Sinai, the mountain of God. Suddenly, the angel of the LORD appeared to him as a blazing fire in a bush. Moses was amazed because the bush was engulfed in flames, but it didn't burn up. "Amazing!" Moses said to himself. "Why isn't that bush burning up? I must go over to see this." When the LORD saw that he had caught Moses' attention, God called to him from the bush, "Moses! Moses!" "Here I am!" Moses replied. "Do not come any closer," God told him. "Take off your sandals, for you are standing on holy ground." Then he said, "I am the God of your ancestors--the God of Abraham, the God of Isaac, and the God of Jacob." When Moses heard this, he hid his face in his hands because he was afraid to look at God.
Exodus 3:1-6

* * *

When this passage begins, Moses is having a "normal" day. He is doing the same thing that he has done almost every day for the past forty years. He did not wake up thinking that he was going to be standing on holy ground before the day was out. That is how most invitations come; that is how most journeys begin.

Moses saw something that day which at first glance was not that unusual. Moses was tending his flock and noticed a bush in the distance that was ablaze. That was a common sight on that part of the mountain at this time of year. The dryness of the earth, combined with the intensity of the sun often caused bushes to burst into flame. But Moses began to notice that the fire was not burning itself out; and what's more, the bush was not being consumed. Having never seen anything like it in his life, he decided to go investigate this phenomenon a little more closely.

As Moses approached the bush, God knew that He had Moses' attention, so He spoke to Moses, revealing Himself and Who He is. There is no indication in Scripture that God had ever spoken to Moses prior to that day. But on that day, Moses knew that he was hearing the voice of the Lord God Jehovah.

God desires for each and every one of His children to know Him, to know Him more and to know Him more intimately. It is God that initiates His activity. It is God's plan that we as His children respond to Him, not the other way around. God will initiate activity in our lives to seize our attention, just as He did through the bush that day. Whether it is a circumstance we encounter, or a situation in which we find ourselves struggling, or a word aptly spoken, or any other of the countless ways that He should choose, God will place in our path that "burning bush" that causes us to turn, walk closer and investigate further. Once He knows that He has our attention, He will speak. As He does He will reveal Himself, Who He is and then extend His invitation. That invitation will always entail leaving where we are and going with Him. Leaving may not always mean a change of geography, but it will always mean leaving the status quo. It will always mean that your life will never be the same. You cannot encounter God and walk away unchanged. As Henry Blackaby says, "God's invitation will require you to make an adjustment to join with Him that will lead to a crisis of belief." That invitation will lead to a journey through the wilderness – that journey through the unknown.

Over five hundred years earlier, God had extended an invitation to Abraham. He told Abraham to take his beloved son, Isaac, to a place God would show him, and there offer him as a burnt sacrifice to God. What Abraham did next is why God commends him for his faith. Abraham did exactly what God told him to do! Abraham knew he had heard God. (God will never leave us in doubt on that point. If you are not sure, ask Him.) i often wonder, as he climbed the mountain with Isaac, as he built the altar, as he bound Isaac's hands and feet, or as he raised the knife to cut Isaac's throat, what questions was he asking? Then at that last moment, God stayed his hand and provided the sacrifice. It was not solely Abraham's

66KENNETH A. WINTER

action that confirmed his faith; it was also God's response to Abraham's faith.

What invitation has God extended to you? You must go forward, trusting God. He will use this journey, not only in your life, but also in your family's lives and in your friends' lives. Imagine Sarah, as she watched what Abraham was doing that day. Imagine Moses' family when he went home and told them what God had told him to do. Many are watching; many are waiting to see what God is going to do through your faithful obedience. He will not forsake you. He will often allow us to come to a place in the journey where everything appears the bleakest. But that is where His hand will be the most conspicuously seen. Trust Him.

Has He extended an invitation to you to go – to journey with Him through the wilderness? Trust Him. He will stay your hand. He will guide your steps. He has made the path.

* * *

3

LORD, ARE YOU SURE?

*Then the LORD told him, "You can be sure I have seen the misery of my people in
Egypt. I have heard their cries for deliverance from their harsh slave drivers. Yes, I
am aware of their suffering. So I have come to rescue them from the Egyptians and
lead them out of Egypt into their own good and spacious land. It is a land flowing
with milk and honey--the land where the Canaanites, Hittites, Amorites,
Perizzites, Hivites, and Jebusites live. The cries of the people of Israel have reached
me, and I have seen how the Egyptians have oppressed them with heavy tasks.
Now go, for I am sending you to Pharaoh. You will lead my people, the Israelites,
out of Egypt." "But who am I to appear before Pharaoh?" Moses asked God.
"How can you expect me to lead the Israelites out of Egypt?"*
Exodus 3:7-11

* * *

W hy is it when God invites us to journey through the wilderness,
one of our first responses is often, "LORD, are You sure You know
what You are doing?" God had heard the cries of His people and He was
preparing to not only deliver them from their bondage, He was preparing
to do a new work in and through them. He was not only going to rescue
them; He was going to lead them out. Often we want God to rescue us,
but we're not very interested in having Him lead us out – particularly if it
includes a time in the wilderness or will force us to step outside of our
comfort zone. Our mind then begins to race, as we come up with all the
reasons we should not make this journey.

Moses had already demonstrated an alertness to the activity of God. The very fact that he was standing where he was and hearing the voice of God demonstrates a willingness to hear and to heed God's voice. But even he struggled with what God was saying. Moses had lived the first forty years of his life in Pharaoh's palace. He had enjoyed the good life of Egypt. Of course, he had seen the oppression of the people; and his own attempts to rescue them from their oppression had led him to murder an Egyptian and live as a fugitive from Egyptian justice for the next forty years of his life. But this was God. Couldn't God deliver the Israelites from slavery but still allow them to stay in Egypt and enjoy the milk and honey there? i mean, this is God, He can do anything! Why not have the Israelites and the Egyptians change places? The Israelites can rule over the Egyptians. Now that sounds like a good plan to me, and no one has to travel anywhere! Moses can avoid the trip back to Pharaoh and the people can avoid the journey. We don't have to deal with the hazards of the wilderness or the giants in the Promised Land. It sounds like a great plan to me! Besides, LORD, what does the Promised Land have to offer that we don't already have in Egypt? And surely You don't expect me to lead the Israelites out of Egypt through the wilderness?

We all resist taking the journey. Whether our current surroundings are idyllic or intolerable, we are comfortable right where we are. We would much rather have God eliminate the crisis and enable us to stay right where we are, so we can avoid the wilderness. We don't usually mind leaving if we can go straight from here to the Promised Land, provided it's not too much of a stretch for our comfort zone. It's the wilderness we don't want to have anything to do with. And sometimes God permits the suffering in our present surroundings, so that we are willing to leave from where we are, to go with Him. He knows our propensity to want to stay where we are. But He loves us too much to leave us where we are!

Often as we struggle with the thought of leaving, we lose sight of the same thing Moses lost sight of – God is going with us; as a matter of fact, He will be leading us. He has extended an invitation to us to join Him, to follow Him and to journey with Him. He has promised to take us all the way through. Yes, the journey's path is through the wilderness; but didn't God create the wilderness too? And didn't He look back at everything He created and say, "It is good"? So, doesn't that include the wilderness? Isn't it possible that the wilderness is a good thing? Why do we get so intimidated by the wilderness that we overlook that He is Lord over the wilderness as well?

God has extended His invitation to you to join Him on this journey. He will lead you and He will lead you all the way. And yes, He is sure! Follow Him.

* * *

4

THE JOURNEY BEGINS

And that very day the LORD began to lead the people of Israel out of Egypt, division by division. The Israelites took with them their bread dough made without yeast. They wrapped their kneading bowls in their spare clothing and carried them on their shoulders. And the people of Israel did as Moses had instructed and asked the Egyptians for clothing and articles of silver and gold. The LORD caused the Egyptians to look favorably on the Israelites, and they gave the Israelites whatever they asked for.... That night the people of Israel left Rameses and started for Succoth. There were about 600,000 men, plus all the women and children. And they were all traveling on foot.
Exodus 12:51, 34-38

* * *

The Israelites had lived in Egypt for 430 years; as a matter of fact it was 430 years to the day. Now on this day the Lord was leading His people on a journey to a land that He had promised them, a journey that would lead through the wilderness. For centuries they had cried out to God for deliverance. They had known of no other life than the bondage of Egypt. They had heard of the promises that God had given to their ancestors, Abraham, Isaac and Jacob, but they could not imagine that life was ever going to be different. But on this day, they left behind all the encumbrances of life, as they had known it; they were escaping their slavery. God had finally delivered them. As they began their journey, they did so with a huge degree of relief – their bondage was finally over.

But they also began their journey, with some degree of reservation. As difficult as their years in Egypt had been, it was all they had ever known. Today they were venturing out into the unknown. They had no idea what to expect or what they would encounter. At least as long as they worked in Egypt, they were assured of the food and shelter and protection of the greatest nation on earth. Now as they stepped out into the wilderness, they had no idea where they would find food or shelter, or what enemies they might encounter.

Some of the Israelites had built close relationships with some of the Egyptian people. Not every one had mistreated or abused them; some of the people had befriended them. And as they began, though there was a relief over their freedom, there was also a regret over friends that would never be seen again. Each step into their journey took them another step away from friends that they loved.

But there was also an excitement and an expectancy. This day that they had prayed for, that they had cried out for and that they had longed for, was finally here, and they relished what lie ahead in their journey. What would this land flowing with milk and honey, as Moses described it, be like? What opportunities existed for them and their sons and daughters without the threat of the overseers' whips on their backs? The investment of the sweat of their brow would now be for their own behalf and not for the benefit of their Egyptian overlords.

Yes, as they began their journey, they did so with that mixture of relief, reservation, regret and relish. They saw all of the ways that they would benefit from this journey; they saw all the ways that the journey would impact their lives. There was only one problem – they were looking through their own eyes. They were looking at it as a journey that would lead them from Egypt and their escape from slavery, not as a journey that would lead them to encounter God and His person. God wasn't leading them to bring them from a place; He was leading them to bring them to Himself. God was bringing them on a journey that would bring them to a place that would enable them to know Him, know Him more and know Him more intimately. In that journey, He would lead them through the wilderness, because there are some things we are only able to learn in the wilderness. There would be times on the journey that He would teach them as a part of the crowd, because there are some things that God teaches us when we are part of a crowd; but there would be other times when they would be alone with God, because there are some things we can only learn when we get alone with Him.

God made sure that they had everything from Egypt that was necessary for the journey. They didn't have everything they would need; God would take care of that along the way. But He made sure that they had every-thing that they needed from Egypt. And they would see how God had planned all of this out long before they had any idea.

But one more observation – they traveled on foot. It wasn't going to be a fast journey, and it wasn't going to be short. God's journeys are designed to accomplish all He intends. God is not as concerned with the quantity of time, as He is with the quality of the work the journey accomplishes. Follow Him. Walk in obedience with Him and you will arrive at the end of your journey at the exact time He intends – but not before.

Yes, their journey had begun. It was a journey that God would use to impact their lives; but it was also a journey that God would use to impact the world through them. That's how God's journeys are.

Whatever journey you are on, through whatever wilderness God has you in, He will use it to impact your life and to impact the world around you. Trust Him, your journey has begun. He will lead you, if you will let Him.

* * *

OASIS OR OBSTACLE?

When Pharaoh finally let the people go, God did not lead them on the road that runs through Philistine territory, even though that was the shortest way from Egypt to the Promised Land. God said, "If the people are faced with a battle, they might change their minds and return to Egypt." So God led them along a route through the wilderness toward the Red Sea, and the Israelites left Egypt like a marching army.
Exodus 13:17-18

* * *

In their pilgrimage, God lead the Israelites out of Egypt. Initially, there was joy and excitement and relief and anticipation. They had clearly heard from God and seen His hand leading them and guiding them in the journey. There was no question that He had made the way. There was no question that He had ordered their steps. As they came to the Red Sea it appeared to be a good place to rest and be refreshed; a place to stop and enjoy the cool breeze and the green grasses – an oasis. There they could contemplate the blessings that awaited them in the Promised Land. There they could rest from the weariness of the challenges that had preceded their exodus from Egypt and watch to see how God was going to lead them to the other side.

But soon the oasis turned into an obstacle as the enemy appeared, threatening an overwhelming attack. Defeat threatened them at their back door, their provisions appeared to be insufficient to overcome the enemy and it appeared that God had abandoned them. The oasis before them now appeared to obstruct them from experiencing the blessings that God had for them. And even worse, it appeared that God had forsaken them to experience defeat in the wilderness.

But the oasis was also the instrument God would use to accomplish His blessing. That which the people now saw as a barrier of defeat, God saw (and preordained) to be an instrument of His glory. The Red Sea was always intended by God to be a blessing – never a curse – a blessing to His people and a blessing to the nations – as He would use it to bring glory to His Name throughout the world. What changed the Israelites' view of the Red Sea from oasis to obstacle – their circumstances or their perspective? God's perspective looked at the same set of circumstances and saw an oasis that could be used to refresh His people in a way beyond anything they could imagine – an oasis through which He would bring them to a greater intimacy with Him, a greater fervency in their worship of Him, and a greater testimony of His glory through them.

So how are you looking at the Red Sea before you? Do you see it as the oasis of blessing that your heavenly Father intends or as an obstacle? Yes, the Promised Land does await you on the other side, but you will not cross through the Red Sea until such time as God intends. He has a purpose for it. He desires to bless you right where you are. He desires to use this Red Sea in your life to bring you to a greater intimacy with Him, a greater fervency in your worship of Him, and use the circumstance to bring greater testimony of His glory. Only He can make a way through the sea. He has ordered your steps to it; He has not ordered your steps to go around it; and only He can order your steps through it.

Yes, He placed the Red Sea before you. Enjoy the oasis, experience the blessings that He has for you through it, and watch the deliverance of the Lord.

* * *

THE PLACE WHERE THE REEDS GROW

Then the LORD gave these instructions to Moses: "Tell the people to march toward Pi-hahiroth between Migdol and the sea. Camp there along the shore, opposite Baal-zephon. Then Pharaoh will think, 'Those Israelites are confused. They are trapped between the wilderness and the sea!' And once again I will harden Pharaoh's heart, and he will chase after you. I have planned this so I will receive great glory at the expense of Pharaoh and his armies. After this, the Egyptians will know that I am the LORD!" So the Israelites camped there as they were told.
Exodus 14:1-4

* * *

A s you journey across your wilderness, God will lead you toward your Pi-hahiroth ("the place where the reeds grow"). It lies on the west bank of your Red Sea, between Migdol (the high place or "watchtower") and the sea and is opposite from Baal-zephon (that place where the idol of this world is worshiped). It will appear to those watching that you are confused or disoriented, but take heart – the LORD has lead you to the place where He will receive great glory.

He has not led you to Migdol - the high place - to the mountaintop. He knows that we would be tempted to stay there and bask in His glory, just as Peter, James and John were at the Mount of Transfiguration. No, He is our High Tower and He has plans for us down in the valley through which He will receive greater glory.

He has led you to a place that is opposite of Baal-zephon - where the world would go. He has not led you on this journey to covet (or worship) the things that this world has to offer. He has brought us to a place that we not be distracted by the things of this world, reminding us that we are not to seek those things, but to seek Him. (Beware that the world will not understand, for they dwell in Baal-zephon and they seek the ways of the world.)

No, He has led you to Pi-hahiroth – the place where the reeds grow. The ground is right for just that purpose. The reed is not known for its strength – for it has none - or for its beauty. It is a tall, coarse grass with few distinguishing features. No, there is nothing special about the reed. But look what the Master can do with that reed. He can turn it into a musical instrument, through which He can make beautiful melodies of praise. He can turn it into an arrow, which He can use to defeat His enemy or carry His message to others. Just as the Egyptians used the papyrus reed to make paper, He can turn the reed into a palette on which He can write His story of His glory. He can take that reed together with other reeds and form a weaving frame on which He will weave His beautiful tapestry. Yes, left to it's own devices, the reed can do nothing, but in the hands of the Master, the reed becomes an instrument of His glory. And the Master determines when the reed is ready to be used, and just how to use it.

God has led you to Pi-hahiroth – the place where the reeds grow. As Paul wrote, "God deliberately chose things the world considers … powerless to shame those who are powerful" and "things, counted as nothing at all, and used them to bring to nothing what the world considers important, so that no one can ever boast in the presence of God." He has you just where He wants you that He might use you as an instrument of His glory – even on this side of the Red Sea. He has planned this so that He will receive great glory and that the world may know that He is the LORD. Camp here as He has told you, until He leads you to the other side.

* * *

DON'T JUST DO SOMETHING, STAND THERE

But Moses told the people, "Don't be afraid. Just stand where you are and watch the LORD rescue you. The Egyptians that you see today will never be seen again. The LORD himself will fight for you. You won't have to lift a finger in your defense!" ...Early in the morning, the LORD looked down on the Egyptian army from the pillar of fire and cloud, and he threw them into confusion. Their chariot wheels began to come off, making their chariots impossible to drive. "Let's get out of here!" the Egyptians shouted. "The LORD is fighting for Israel against us!" ... When the people of Israel saw the mighty power that the LORD had displayed against the Egyptians, they feared the LORD and put their faith in him and his servant Moses.
Exodus 14:13-14, 24-25, 31

* * *

Just stand where you are and watch the LORD rescue you. Did anyone ever say to you – "Don't just stand there, do something"? We are raised with that admonition from childhood – that as long as we remain in motion, everything will work out. We've even spiritualized it with the statement – "God helps those who help themselves." (i venture to guess that many of us actually believe that is a verse in the Bible.) And yet, throughout time God has said to His people, stand still and see the deliverance of the Lord.

Imagine the scene. Men, women and children; young and old; raised to be slaves – field workers, domestics and construction workers – they had never received any training in combat - and pursuing them was the fiercest and mightiest army in the world – the best of the best. As the Israelites took inventory of their weapons, they paled in comparison with the weapons of warfare being wielded by their opposing force. Their carts drawn by their weary oxen were no match for the rapidly approaching chariots drawn by horses that had been bred for war. Their intimidation quickly turned to fear and then to panic. Seeing the desperation of their situation, they did two things: first, they cried out to the Lord to help them, and second, they turned against Moses – accusing him of leading them into the wilderness to die.

Their cry to the Lord to help them was similar to the cry of the disciples that night in the boat to Jesus to wake up and help them. It was a cry for God to help them with their feeble plan – their lame attempt to take things in their own hands and ask God to bless it. And as they turned against Moses, they set aside God's promise to deliver them into His land of promise. His promise was not a call to the wilderness; His promise was to a land that would first require them to go through the wilderness. The One who had led them this far would lead them all the way!

What have you encountered in the wilderness? What enemy is threatening to overtake you in the journey that God has led you in? The obstacle or enemy will be greater than anything that you are able to overcome, because God intends to use it for His glory – glory through the eyes of a watching world, and glory through the faith that is grown in your life as you trust Him and see His deliverance. God's work was so conspicuous that the Egyptian army proclaimed it and the Israelites feared Him and put their faith in Him.

Trust His Person, His presence, His power and His promise. Don't just do something, stand there and watch the Lord deliver you.

* * *

8

A "SHUR" WAY

*Then Moses led the people of Israel away from the Red Sea, and they moved out
into the Shur Desert. They traveled in this desert for three days without water.
When they came to Marah, they finally found water. But the people couldn't
drink it because it was bitter. (That is why the place was called Marah, which
means "bitter.") Then the people turned against Moses. "What are we going to
drink?" they demanded.
So Moses cried out to the LORD for help, and the LORD showed him a branch.
Moses took the branch and threw it into the water. This made the water good
to drink.*
Exodus 15:22-25

* * *

I t took just three days. On, let's say it was Monday, they were singing
His praises – "Who is glorious in holiness like You – so awesome in
splendor, performing such wonders?" (Vs. 11) Then by Thursday they had
turned against Him. On Monday they had experienced one of the greatest
miracles of God, but by Thursday they had again lost hope. On Monday
they had walked through walls of water without even getting their feet
wet, but by Thursday they were crying out that they had been left to die of
thirst.

As the people walked away from the Red Sea, they moved through the
Shur Desert, or the Wilderness of Shur. The name "Shur" means walled
enclosure. On Monday, God had led them through a walled enclosure of

water; and for the three days thereafter He had led His people through a walled enclosure of wilderness. God's way was straight; God's way was sure. He provided the walls surrounding their way in order to direct them and protect them. As long as they walked in His way, they were assured of His presence, His protection, His provision and His power. And they could be assured that though enemies and circumstances might enter their path that would threaten to defeat them, He had permitted that intrusion for the sole purpose that He might demonstrate His glory through them. He had allowed the Egyptian army to enter the walls of water through the Red Sea that they might be defeated for His glory. And now He had allowed Marah (bitter waters) to enter their way through the wilderness for that same purpose. Was the God who was able to defeat the one enemy on Monday able to overcome the other on Thursday? Was the God who had declared Himself to be their God, who had promised to redeem them, deliver them and lead them able to see them through any and every hardship or trial? Did that include the bitter waters of Marah?

How quickly we too forget – that the God of Abraham, Isaac and Jacob, the God who turned the bitter waters sweet, is the same God who has promised to never leave us or forsake us. He is the same God who has promised to make our way straight and sure. He has ordered our steps before us and made a way in the wilderness. And we can walk in His assurance that nothing can enter into that way that He has not permitted, and if He has permitted it, He has done so with the assurance that He will use it to His glory and for our good. There is nothing too minor and there is nothing too big. And that promise is not only for Monday; that promise is also for Thursday and every other day.

Let us remember that God took that bitter water, that bitter circumstance, and didn't just make it drinkable or palatable – He made it good. You see, whatever God transforms, He transforms it to good. That is the assurance that Paul writes about in Romans 8:28. Everything that God ever created or transformed, He has declared to be good.

So, let us continue to boldly walk in the path that He has set our feet upon – His "Shur" way for us – with a confidence that as we walk in His way, our way is sure!

* * *

THE PROMISE OF ELIM

It was there at Marah that the LORD laid before them the following conditions to test their faithfulness to him: "If you will listen carefully to the voice of the LORD your God and do what is right in his sight, obeying his commands and laws, then I will not make you suffer the diseases I sent on the Egyptians; for I am the LORD who heals you." After leaving Marah, they came to Elim, where there were twelve springs and seventy palm trees. They camped there beside the springs.
Exodus 15:25-27

* * *

I t had been a week – and what a week it had been! The preceding weeks had seen the plagues that God had brought upon Egypt, culminating with the death of Egypt's firstborn sons. The week had begun with the pronouncement from Pharaoh that the people were to leave Egypt – leave quickly - they were free of the bondage they had suffered for generations. They had seen God part the Red Sea - no one would forget that eerie walk from west to east through the walls of water or the sight as they stood on the eastern shore as those walls came crashing down upon the pursuing Egyptian army. And now they had seen God transform the bitter waters into sweet. They had experienced the roller coaster of emotions from elation, joy, exuberance and awe to fear, panic, bitterness and anger – and back again – and back again some more. They had experienced God's presence and protection and provision in ways that just one week earlier they could not even have imagined – and they had seen Him demonstrate His awesome power. God was now preparing to lead them to the beautiful valley of Elim – the valley of strong trees – with its twelve deep natural springs of fresh sweet water – one spring for each of the twelve tribes of Israel. But before He did so, the God of Abraham, Isaac and Jacob was setting before His people the conditions under which they were to follow Him – they were to listen for His voice, heed His voice and obey His voice.

The psalmist wrote in the first Psalm: *"Blessed is the man who walks not in the counsel of the ungodly, nor stands in the path of sinners, nor sits in the seat of the scornful; but his delight is in the law of the LORD, and in His law he meditates day and night. He shall be like a tree planted by the rivers of water, that brings forth its fruit in its season, whose leaf also shall not wither; and whatever he does shall prosper."* Here again we see God telling His people that if they will meditate on His word (listen for His voice), delight in His word (heed His voice), and walk according to His word (obey His voice) they will be like strong trees planted by deep water – trees that will prosper and bring forth fruit.

God gave them a promise with a condition while they were still in Marah, then He led them to Elim. Elim was a picture of what His people would be if they heeded His voice – it was a visual reminder of His promise – they would be like those strong trees firmly planted beside the deep water. God kept the Israelites encamped in Elim for several weeks so that they might be refreshed for the continuation of their journey, but also so that this reminder of His promise might be etched on their hearts.

Jesus gave us the same promise when He said, *"I am the Vine, you are the branches. He who abides in Me, and I in him, bears much fruit; for without Me you can do nothing"* (John 15:5). If we are going to abide in Him, we must listen for His voice, heed His voice and obey His voice. As we do, He will bear fruit in us and through us – fruit that remains – fruit that is sufficient for the journey – and we can know that our way will prosper. Allow the Master to use this picture of Elim to challenge you, to refresh you and to remind you, as He leads you in your journey through the wilderness.

* * *

THE WILDERNESS OF SIN

Then they left Elim and journeyed into the Sin Desert, between Elim and Mount Sinai. They arrived there a month after leaving Egypt. There, too, the whole community of Israel spoke bitterly against Moses and Aaron. "Oh, that we were back in Egypt," they moaned. "It would have been better if the LORD had killed us there! At least there we had plenty to eat. But now you have brought us into this desert to starve us to death."
Exodus 16:1-3

* * *

G od had promised Moses at the burning bush that he would return to Mount Sinai with the people to worship Him. Having enjoyed a season of refreshment at Elim, the Israelites now continued on their journey to Mount Sinai, traveling through the Wilderness of Sin. "Sin" was the Egyptian name meaning "moon-god" and is indicative of the Egyptian's pagan worship and false beliefs – beliefs that were in opposition and in disobedience to the law and the Person of God – what God calls (in the English language) "sin".

How often do we find ourselves traveling through the wilderness of sin? As a matter-of-fact we have probably all traveled from Elim to Sinai through the wilderness of sin. You remember – it was Sunday morning. You had just awakened from a refreshing night's sleep (your Elim) and were preparing to go to church to corporately worship God (your Sinai) and enroute someone said something or did something and you found yourself responding in such a way that there was no question you were smack-dab in the middle of the wilderness of sin. (Yes, loosen your halo – we've all been there!) The way you and i act in the wilderness of sin is the same way the Israelites responded.

First, they took their eyes off of the One who was leading them. God was bringing them to the mountain that they might worship Him. God created us to worship Him. He is worthy of our worship. Our very lives are to be an offering of worship. When we set our eyes on Him, like the apostle John in the Revelation we will fall at His feet and worship Him. There will be no other response if our eyes are on Him. But in the midst of the journey, they, like us, took their eyes off of Him.

When they did, they became distracted by their circumstances and their surroundings. When we take our eyes off of our Lord, we become disoriented – we lose sight of not only His Person, but also His purpose and His plan – and we start to think that it is all about us. We start to think about our comfort and our convenience. And when we do, the wilderness ceases to be a path to worship and becomes an uncomfortable and inconvenient place to be. The walk through it is too long, too hot and too difficult.

And then what do we do? Just like the Israelites, we begin to murmur. We begin to complain and rationalize our behavior. We often even try and spiritualize our murmuring. "I'm a child of God. Surely He doesn't expect me to suffer this way. I'm going to leave this church and go to one that appreciates me more…, or one that better meets my needs."

And the next thing we know, we are hungering for the things of this world. Those leaks and onions back in Egypt never tasted better. We have become so blinded by our fleshly desires that we are ready to return to the captivity that this world has to offer in order to receive the temporary satisfaction that those things will provide.

Are you finding yourself sliding down the slippery slope of the wilderness of sin in the midst of your wilderness journey? Turn your eyes back to the One who has led you there. He is leading you in a journey of worship. Look to His Person. Remember His promise. Trust His purpose.

He will see you through the journey. He will meet every need. Even though you can't see the end of the journey, He has it in sight. Just follow Him.

* * *

11

COMPLAINTS THAT DENY

Then the LORD said to Moses, "Look, I'm going to rain down food from heaven for you. The people can go out each day and pick up as much food as they need for that day..."
Then Moses and Aaron called a meeting of all the people of Israel and told them, "In the evening you will realize that it was the LORD who brought you out of the land of Egypt. In the morning you will see the glorious presence of the LORD. He has heard your complaints, which are against the LORD and not against us. The LORD will give you meat to eat in the evening and bread in the morning, for he has heard all your complaints against him. Yes, your complaints are against the LORD, not against us."
Exodus 16:4, 6-8

* * *

It had been a month since they left Egypt. Imagine the food supplies that had been needed to keep this group of well over one million people fed for thirty days. My wife and i have a teenage son who eats just one meal a day – it starts when he wakes up and concludes when he goes to bed at night. Sprinkle a few teenage boys in that crowd and you're talking some food! The provision of food that they had brought from Egypt was now exhausted – and the people were hungry. There they were in the desert with no food, nowhere to get it and empty stomachs. And we read, *"The whole community spoke bitterly against Moses and Aaron."* That sounds like an understatement – i'm picturing a lynch mob of one million plus! Instead of praising the One who, to this point, had provided for their every need, had protected them from every danger, and had piloted them through every turn, they rose up in one voice to complain about the problem instead of seeking His solution. Their complaints, though directed at Moses and Aaron, were really against God. And through their complaints, they were denying the faithfulness of God!

But God was faithful – even to this group of ungrateful complainers. He promised that He would deliver bread in the morning and meat in the evening, in quantities sufficient for the day. He would provide enough that everyone would receive their fill. No one would go hungry. All they needed to do was go out and pick it up.

And not only would God's provision meet their need; it would be a testimony to His faithfulness. In the evening it would be a reminder that He had delivered them from their bondage, and in the morning that He had delivered them into His glorious presence.

This was to be a visual reminder to the Israelites, and a testimony to us, that God's tender mercies and His compassion are new every morning and sufficient for the day (Lam 3:23-24). That there is no need that we will ever have that He is not able to meet – and He will do so in ways that are beyond what we could ask or think to bring glory to His name to all generations. When our need is tied to His purpose, we are doubly assured of His provision for the sake of the glory of His Name. Remember, God had chosen this people so that through them all the nations of the world would be blessed. God will withhold no good thing from His children so that all the nations of the world may know that He is God and there is no other. And *"the people will declare, 'The LORD is the source of all my right-eousness and strength.' And all who were angry with Him will come to Him and be ashamed... and in Him they will boast"* (Isa 45:24-25).

What do you have need of as you follow your Lord in the wilderness? Will you deny His faithfulness and complain? Or will you declare His faithfulness and experience His tender mercies new each day? He who has begun this good work will be faithful to complete it!

* * *

SEEN THE CLOUD? SEE THE GLORY!

Then Moses said to Aaron, "Say this to the entire community of Israel: 'Come into the LORD's presence, and hear his reply to your complaints.'" And as Aaron spoke to the people, they looked out toward the desert. Within the guiding cloud, they could see the awesome glory of the LORD.
Exodus 16:9-10

* * *

T he LORD had given His people a constant reminder of His presence from the first day of their journey. He had set a pillar of cloud to go before them by day, and a pillar of fire by night. That way they could travel by day or night, and never lose sight of where and how He was leading. And in Exodus 13:22 we read, *"And the LORD did not remove the pillar of cloud or pillar of fire from their sight."* This visible reminder had been there for the entire month since their journey began. The cloud had gone before them as they camped at Pi-hahiroth; it had gone behind them to protect them as the Egyptian army threatened their attack. It had led them to Marah and to Elim And now the LORD continued to guide their steps even through the Wilderness of Sin. But even with this constant reminder of His presence before them, the people were grumbling and complaining. Though He was going before them and He had never removed His presence from their sight, they had become blinded to His presence.

Their sins of rebelliousness, faithlessness, bitterness, and anger had blinded them to the reality of His presence, had deafened them to the reminder of His promise, and had hardened them against the confidence of His purpose. That's what sin does – it blinds us, it deafens us, it hardens us and it separates us from the God who loves us and envelopes us in His presence. Though He was right there, they could no longer see Him for Who He was. So Moses said to them through Aaron, "Come into His presence." In essence He was saying, "Turn from yourselves; turn from those things that you have allowed to blind you and distract you and capture your attention – and turn to the LORD."

He has heard your complaints; now hear His reply. Have you become convinced that you are going to perish, or that this journey will end in disaster? You have looked at your circumstances and tried to determine the reality of your situation. The reality of your situation is that you do not know the reality of your situation until you have heard from God. More often than not, He's not going to tell you what you want to hear; but He is always going to tell you what you need to hear! And as you hear His voice, He will require a response from you – He will require that you make an adjustment from where you are.

And as Aaron spoke to the people, they turned from their tents – from themselves – and turned toward the desert where the pillar of cloud stood before them. And their eyes were opened – for within the cloud appeared the awesome glory of the LORD.

As you travel on your wilderness journey, have you become blinded to the reality of His presence? Have you allowed unconfessed sin to linger in your heart and distract your attention to your circumstances? Or have you allowed your circumstances to spiral out of control due to your uncon-fessed sin? He hasn't left you. He hasn't abandoned you. He's always been there. The answer is as simple as it was to the Israelites that day. Turn your heart back toward Him. Turn from yourself and turn to Him. Repent of your sin and turn to Him – and you, too, will again see His awesome glory going before you.

* * *

13

THE LESSON OF THE QUAIL

And the LORD said to Moses, "I have heard the people's complaints. Now tell them, 'In the evening you will have meat to eat, and in the morning you will be filled with bread. Then you will know that I am the LORD your God.' " That evening vast numbers of quail arrived and covered the camp.
Exodus 16:11-13

* * *

Everything that God does, reveals His divine nature. He had seized their attention through their natural need – their need for food. Their eyes were now turned to Him; their ears were now trained on Him. Now that He had the full attention of His people, God was prepared to meet their natural need in His supernatural way.

Do you remember when God appeared to Moses through the burning bush? God did not speak to Moses until he had turned his complete attention to God. Such is the case here. God was preparing to meet their need in just such a way that the people might again know that He is God – their God – and they are not. And He would do nothing until He had their complete attention.

Does that mean that God was not at work until the Israelites turned their attention back to Him? Never! God was making preparations for their deliverance even before they realized they had need. Let's look at the miracle of the quail. Quail begin their migration from Equatorial Africa to Europe and Western Asia in the Spring. Based upon the average flying speed of the quail, it would have taken them approximately three days to travel from Africa to the Wilderness of Sin. God promised His people that they would have meat to eat that evening. That means that He had already set in motion the events to deliver it to them at least two days prior.

Secondly, the Wilderness of Sin lays east of the migratory corridor of the quail, which means that God shifted the prevailing winds during their migration to deliver them right to the Israelites' camp – a reminder that God will move heaven and earth to accomplish His purpose and fulfill His promise.

Thirdly, imagine the number of quail required to provide the Israelites with their fill of fowl. If you have ever seen the Alfred Hitchcock movie "The Birds", the quantity of birds reflected in that movie pales in comparison to the flock that arrived in the Israelite's camp that evening. God timed their arrival by night because the sheer volume of birds in the sky would have blotted out the sun. And having just finished their winter feed, these quail were large and plump. God provided all that was required to meet their need.

So what are the lessons learned in the wilderness through the quail? First, God has promised to meet our every need as we follow Him on this wilderness journey; there is no need too large and none too small. Second, He will use His provision to bring glory to His Name. Therefore, we will not see nor experience His full provision until we have given Him our complete attention. Third, God will accomplish it all in His perfect time and in His perfect way – moving heaven and earth, if need be, to accomplish it. Fourth, He will meet our need in ways that are beyond anything that we could plan, hope or even imagine.

As you journey across your wilderness, remember the lesson of the quail and trust Him.

* * *

14

WHAT IS IT?

"I have heard the people's complaints. Now tell them, 'In the evening you will have meat to eat, and in the morning you will be filled with bread. Then you will know that I am the LORD your God.'" ...The next morning the desert all around the camp was wet with dew. When the dew disappeared later in the morning, thin flakes, white like frost, covered the ground. The Israelites were puzzled when they saw it. "What is it?" they asked. And Moses told them, "It is the food the LORD has given you."
Exodus 16:12-15

* * *

G od promised His people that in the morning they would be filled with bread. That night they experienced a feast of fowl delivered fresh to their doorstep. They had never tasted meat so good; nor experienced it in the quantities that God had provided that night. It was truly a feast that was infinitely more than they could have hoped for or asked.

After what God had provided that night, can you imagine the expectancy that the people had for what He was going to do in the morning? They could envision bread that was beyond anything that they had ever had. The fragrant aroma of fresh bread baking was already filling their nostrils. The sweet taste of warm fresh-baked bread was already making their taste buds salivate. Not only did they believe that God was going to provide and trust Him to do so, they could now picture the bountiful way in which He was going to do so. They had a picture in their mind based upon His promise; they already had a praise on their lips based upon that picture.

i wonder how the people slept that night. Did they stay awake with the same excitement and expectancy of a child awaiting the arrival of Christmas morning? Did they set their "wake-up alarm" a little earlier so that they could be one of the first to see God's provision? As the first glimmer of the sunrise appeared on the horizon, did they quickly arise and look all about for God's morning delivery? Did they look to the sky to see if God's bread was falling from the ovens of heaven just as the quail had the night before? Did they look to the coal fires that they had used to roast the quail to see if God had delivered the bread to these same fires to bake? But everywhere they looked, they didn't see bread. All they saw around them was the wet morning dew – and they had seen that every morning. What was going on? God had promised! God had always been faithful to accomplish what He promised. Where was the aroma? Where were those fresh loaves?

i can imagine the people turning to Moses and Aaron for explanation. i can imagine the bewildered looks. Had they heard God correctly or had they misunderstood? It was morning and there was no bread. Then one of the "more godly" in the crowd said, "Yes, but morning isn't over. Morning goes until noon – and God is always right on time and never late! Watch and see. It just hasn't arrived yet."

As the morning went on and the people continued to watch and wait, the dew began to disappear. Someone noticed that where the dew had evaporated, there remained a thin white layer of crust. They had never seen that before. One neighbor pointed it out to the next and pretty soon their curiosity got the better of them so they walked toward it to investigate. Someone reached down, broke off a piece and picked it up. It didn't feel like anything they had ever felt before. They smelled it – it didn't smell like anything they ever smelled before. Then someone – you know, there's one in every crowd – tasted it, and it didn't taste like anything they'd ever tasted before. And then in one voice they asked Moses, "What is it?" And Moses said, "It is the food that God has promised you."

"Oh no, this can't be God's provision. It doesn't look, smell, taste or feel anything like I thought it would. It doesn't pass the test of my senses or line up with my expectations. Surely this isn't God's provision."

As you journey in the wilderness today, watch for God's provision – but be mindful as you do that His ways are not your ways! Is your trust based upon His promise or your picture of it?

* * *

15

BREAD THAT IS SUFFICIENT

"I have heard the people's complaints. Now tell them, 'In the evening you will have meat to eat, and in the morning you will be filled with bread. Then you will know that I am the LORD your God.'" ...And Moses told them, "It is the food the LORD has given you. The LORD says that each household should gather as much as it needs. Pick up two quarts for each person." So the people of Israel went out and gathered this food -- some getting more, and some getting less. By gathering two quarts for each person, everyone had just enough. Those who gathered a lot had nothing left over, and those who gathered only a little had enough. Each family had just what it needed. Then Moses told them, "Do not keep any of it overnight." But, of course, some of them didn't listen and kept some of it until morning. By then it was full of maggots and had a terrible smell.
Exodus 16:12, 15-20

* * *

God promised that each morning He would provide bread that would be sufficient for every person for the day – each would have his or her fill. After the people had gotten over the shock that this "white, flaky stuff" was God's bread for them, they set about the process of gathering what was needed for their household. God's provision, though "packaged" in a very unexpected way, came with very specific instruction. He gave them a specific quantity to collect for each person. Each household was not to collect the same quantity – it would vary based upon the size of their family, but they would receive the same proportion. God reiterated through Moses' instruction that as each household followed His instruction their need would be fully met – they would have just enough.

God promised that His provision would be unending (until He said otherwise) and would be sufficient for each day – He would meet today's need today, and tomorrow's need tomorrow. His provision was assured – not because of what He had provided, but because of what He had promised. And as they followed His instruction, each family had just what they needed.

Lest there be any confusion, Moses admonished them, "Do not try and horde God's provision. Do not try and keep any of it overnight." God's provision is predicated on His promise and our obedience to His instruction. There were some who would not listen; some whose trust was in themselves and their abilities to collect more, consume less and conserve for tomorrow. Are those abilities or actions wrong? No, unless they are in direct disobedience to God. They were placing their faith and trust in their ability and not in God and they were directly disobeying His command. In essence, they were saying, "God, You were able to provide today, but You may not be able to provide tomorrow, so I'm going to help You out." And the result was the same that occurs whenever we disobey God – maggots and malodor – the fruit of death and decay.

If you are journeying in the wilderness, God has promised to provide all that you need; and He has promised to do so in a way that you will know – as will a watching world – that He is Jehovah Jireh – the Lord who provides. His provision is a part of His purpose that will lead to His glory. If you are His child, He has chosen you to be an instrument though whom He makes His Name known. Therefore, heed the instruction He has given you. Be obedient in all that He has set before you to do. Do not take matters into your own hands. God never said that He helps those who help themselves. That's the principle that led to maggots and malodor. Do not slack from what He has told you to do. Heed His instruction – be faithful and diligent. Remember that His provision is assured – not because of what He has provided in the past, but because of what He has promised. And if you will trust Him, you, too, will find that His provision will be fully sufficient for the day.

* * *

16

PUT TO THE TEST

Then the LORD said to Moses, "Look, I'm going to rain down food from heaven for you. The people can go out each day and pick up as much food as they need for that day. I will test them in this to see whether they will follow my instructions. Tell them to pick up twice as much as usual on the sixth day of each week." ...The people gathered the food morning by morning, each family according to its need. ...On the sixth day, there was twice as much as usual on the ground -- four quarts for each person instead of two. The leaders of the people came and asked Moses why this had happened. He replied, "The LORD has appointed tomorrow as a day of rest, a holy Sabbath to the LORD. On this day we will rest from our normal daily tasks. So bake or boil as much as you want today, and set aside what is left for tomorrow." ...Some of the people went out anyway to gather food, even though it was the Sabbath day. But there was none to be found.
Exodus 16:4-5, 21-23, 27

* * *

E very student knows that once you have been given instruction, you will be given an opportunity to apply that instruction or demonstrate how well you have retained that instruction through a test. Those tests can come in a variety of forms. There are pop quizzes – a few short questions placed before you unexpectedly to test your grasp of an idea, principle or fact soon after it has been presented to you. There are tests – periodic exams given at the conclusion of a defined period of teaching, i.e. weekly, end-of-chapter, etc. And there are exams, including the matriarch of all exams – the final exam – on which you are tested on instruction you have received over a cumulative period. The teachers that I always appre-

ciated the most were the ones that forewarned, "This is going to be on the
test. You need to know this." There was no question that you needed to
study and remember that principle and be able to apply it. There were no
surprises; you either heeded your teacher's admonition or you did not. If
you did, you had a greater probability of passing the test than if you
did not.

Well, God was teaching His children. He was teaching them Who He is.
He was teaching them His character. He was giving them truth to live by;
truth on which they could depend. As every successful teacher knows,
good teaching includes verbal instruction, visual reinforcement, practical
application, personal application and repetition. You see this pattern
repeated throughout Scripture. You see it repeatedly demonstrated
throughout the Gospels as Jesus taught His disciples – He would teach a
truth, demonstrate its application by use of a parable, give them an opportunity to apply the truth to a specific situation and take them through the
process again.

God said, "I'm going to rain down food. Go out each day and pick up
what you need for that day. And on the sixth day, pick up a double
portion. And, by the way, i'm going to test you in this to see if you will
follow My instructions." Consistent with the pattern that He had already
set at the creation, God was instructing His people to set aside a day of
rest each week – a holy Sabbath to the Lord – a day which would be set
apart from all the others unto Him. And so that they would not spend that
day gathering food, He was giving them a double portion on the sixth day
to provide for that Sabbath day.

So how did the people do with the test? Well, some of them throughout
the week tried to horde food from one day to the next. The result – failure
– their effort resulted in maggots and decay. Others of them decided that
they would ignore God's instruction and take advantage of less competi-
tion being in the fields on the seventh day. Their result – failure – their
effort yielded absolutely no harvest. And though I'm sure that both of
these groups intended that no one else know of their disobedience, the
stench of decaying manna or their activity on the day when everyone else
was resting did not go unnoticed. God had given instruction so that
through it, He would be glorified. And the saddest result for those who
failed the test, was not the shame and embarrassment of their disobedience; it was their failure to honor the One who is worthy of all honor.

Along your journey through the wilderness, the One who is leading you will allow you to be put to the test. He is teaching you Who He is, His character and His Truth. Follow His instruction – His Word – and you will pass with flying colors. And He will get the glory – after all, that's why He has you on this journey to begin with.

* * *

17

A MEMORIAL TO THE GIVER, NOT
THE GIFT

In time, the food became known as manna. It was white like coriander seed, and it tasted like honey cakes. Then Moses gave them this command from the LORD: "Take two quarts of manna and keep it forever as a treasured memorial of the LORD's provision. By doing this, later generations will be able to see the bread that the LORD provided in the wilderness when he brought you out of Egypt." ... So the people of Israel ate manna for forty years until they arrived in the land of Canaan, where there were crops to eat.
Exodus 16:31-32, 35

* * *

The word "manna" in Hebrew means "what is it?" – a reasonable name for a substance that the Israelites had never seen before and no one has seen since. It is derived from the Hebrew word "manan" which means "an allotment" or "gift". It could be baked on the ashes or boiled in pots, ground in a mill or beaten in a mortar, or cooked in pans or made into cakes. It was harvested six days a week by the Israelites by simply walking into the desert and collecting a sufficient quantity for that day, or for two days on the sixth day of the week. Every morning after the dew disappeared, there it would be. And it would remain until everyone had harvested his or her portion for the day, then the remainder, which had not been picked up, would simply melt and disappear. This manna, which no one to this point had ever tasted, now became the basic staple of their diet.

And God commanded through Moses that a sample of manna, the "bread of heaven" as described by the psalmist, be set aside and forever kept as a memorial and a reminder to all future generations. It was to be a reminder and a memorial of God's faithfulness and of His provision. Where there was nothing, He had provided. No matter where they were, He had provided. Wherever He led, He had provided. Six days a week for forty years, until there was no further need, He had provided. They could do nothing to make manna. They could do nothing to earn manna. They could do nothing to save manna. It was an expression of God's grace to His people. It was to be kept and remembered as a treasured memorial.

That's how God's provision is. He provides where there is nothing. His provision is sufficient for the day and for the need. His provision is not predicated on our merit or our deservedness, it is a condition of His faithfulness. His provision is not something we can bank for a future day, His provision is such that we can bank that He will be sufficient for that future day. His provision is not our wage or a reward for our faithfulness; it is the product of His faithfulness. He does not provide so that we might merely accumulate possessions, He provides sufficient for the journey that He has led us in. He has not provided for our purpose, but for His. And He will provide for whatever period is required by Him to accomplish His plan. His provision will meet our need. His provision will satisfy and fill us. What more did the Israelites need? What more do we need?

Oh, yes, as you continue your journey in the wilderness, set aside a portion of the manna that He has provided for you, that it too might be a reminder and a memorial of His faithful provision for you in this journey. It is a memorial to the One who gave the provision, and not to the provision itself. Lest you forget when you enter into His promised land for you, that it is He who has led you there, and it is He that through His faithfulness has enabled you to be there.

* * *

18

MERIBAH OR EMUNAH? WHICH WILL IT BE?

At the LORD's command, the people of Israel left the Sin Desert and moved from place to place. Eventually they came to Rephidim, but there was no water to be found there. So once more the people grumbled and complained to Moses. "Give us water to drink!" they demanded. "Quiet!" Moses replied. "Why are you arguing with me? And why are you testing the LORD?" But tormented by thirst, they continued to complain, "Why did you ever take us out of Egypt? Why did you bring us here? We, our children, and our livestock will all die!" Then Moses pleaded with the LORD, "What should I do with these people? They are about to stone me!" The LORD said to Moses, "Take your shepherd's staff, the one you used when you struck the water of the Nile. Then call some of the leaders of Israel and walk on ahead of the people. I will meet you by the rock at Mount Sinai. Strike the rock, and water will come pouring out. Then the people will be able to drink." Moses did just as he was told; and as the leaders looked on, water gushed out. Moses named the place Massah--"the place of testing"--and Meribah--"the place of arguing"--because the people of Israel argued with Moses and tested the LORD by saying, "Is the LORD going to take care of us or not?"
Exodus 17:1-7

* * *

God led His people from the Wilderness of Sin to a fertile part of the peninsula called Rephidim, which means "places of rest or refreshment." But, talk about a place that doesn't live up to its name, they couldn't find any water there to drink. Though there was probably luscious vegetation all around them, just like they had seen in Elim, there was no spring to quench their thirst. And we read, "So once more the

people grumbled and complained to Moses." As if Moses could do something about it! Had Moses parted the Red Sea? Had he turned the bitter
water into sweet at Marah? Was it Moses that was providing the manna
every morning – including that very morning? Are you starting to wonder
why these people are not getting this? Are you getting exasperated as you
read this and want to call out to them – "People, H-E-L-L-O, have you
tried calling upon Jehovah – you know, the One who is leading you with
that large pillar of cloud up there in front? What part of 'God is your
Provider' don't you understand? All this grumbling and complaining is
doing is giving you, Moses and everyone around you one giant headache!
i'm not even there; i'm just reading about it, and you're giving me a
headache!"

But as their thirst increased so did the crescendo of their complaints,
including repeated choruses of "Take Us Back To The Slavery In Egypt".
The people were working on their solution to the problem – they were
determining how best to stone Moses. That would have solved everything! At least for Moses!

As i recount what is happening here, albeit "a little tongue in cheek", i am
again reminded that I have done the exact same thing. Time and again
God has faithfully provided, and time and again as i have encountered a
crisis, i am ashamed to confess, He is the last one i have turned to! i have
allowed the dryness of my throat to restrict the blood flow to my brain,
hardening my heart, blinding my eyes and deafening my ears to the
reality that <u>He</u> is my Answer! <u>He</u> is my Source! He is the only one who can
take this situation and use it for my good. Perhaps it is time for me to drop
the stones i was prepared to throw at anyone who got in my sights, and
drop to my knees and call upon the only One who can make a difference.
If God has led me to Rephidim, He intends to refresh me.

i'd like to report that the Israelites came to this reality, turned to the Lord
and experienced, not only His provision, but through it, a greater intimacy
with His Person. But that didn't happen that day. That day they determined in their hearts to test the Lord and defiantly cry out while shaking
their clenched fists, "Is the Lord going to take care of us or not?" But
Moses turned to God and pleaded on behalf of the people. And because of
His promise to Moses, to Abraham, to Isaac, and to Jacob – even to the
people themselves – God provided the water, and the people were able to
drink. God met Moses at the rock by Mount Sinai, and as the people
looked on, the water gushed out. Because of God's promise and His faith-

fulness, the people experienced His blessing – the water; but because of their obstinance and their arrogance, they missed the intimacy of His presence. That place and that time would forever now be remembered as Massah and Meribah – "the place of testing and of arguing" – not Emmanuel – "God with us" or Emunah – "the place of faithfulness". The other unfortunate part of this story is that the people appear to have been content with just experiencing His blessing without experiencing His presence. They were content to settle for that which would only temporarily satisfy instead of the deeper blessing that God desired for them to have through a more intimate relationship with Him.

What about you? Do you thirst for the water that will only temporarily satisfy or do you thirst for that deep drink of Living Water that can only come through an intimate relationship with your Living Lord? The choice that day at Rephidim was much like the choice that day many years later, when the Samaritan woman encountered Jesus at the well. She chose Living Water and left her bucket at the well – never to thirst again. Which will you choose today? Will this place in your life be known as Meribah – the place of arguing – or will it be known as Emunah – the place of faithfulness?

* * *

19

SIGN ME UP FOR ONE OF THOSE STAFFS

Then the LORD asked him, "What do you have there in your hand?" "A shepherd's staff," Moses replied. ...The LORD said to Moses, "Take your shepherd's staff, the one you used when you struck the water of the Nile. ...Strike the rock, and water will come pouring out. Then the people will be able to drink." Moses did just as he was told; and ... water gushed out. ...As long as Moses held up the staff with his hands, the Israelites had the advantage. But whenever he lowered his hands, the Amalekites gained the upper hand.
Exodus 4:2; 17:5-6, 11

* * *

For my journey through the wilderness, i want one of those shepherd's staffs! From that very first day at the burning bush, God had demonstrated His power through that staff. He had turned it into a snake. He had turned the water of the Nile River into blood with it. God had Moses outstretch it to part the waters, and He had him strike a rock with it to bring forth water. Then God used it to ensure a victory in the battle with the Amalekites. Sign me up for one of those staffs!

Wouldn't you like to have a staff that you could use to turn the tide of every trial you encounter? Every time you encounter an obstacle, out comes the staff. It's better than any laser weapon ever devised by those science fiction writers. Every obstacle and every enemy cowers at its mere presence. It's not much to look at but it packs a powerful punch. As a matter of fact, if you're going to get one, why not get two and you can pack double the punch. But why stop there, order a truckload. And do you know what you've got when you've got a truckload of staffs? Yes, that's right – you've got a whole lot - - - of wood!

You and i both know there was no power in that staff. It was merely an instrument – a tool – that God chose to use in the hands of His servant. It was an outward expression of the power of God manifested through His servant, through which He intended to bring Himself glory. That's why the consequence for Moses was so severe when later He misused the staff God had given him – but i'm getting ahead of myself.

Look again, at how that staff came to be used. Moses had been tending Jethro's flocks with it for almost forty years. For all that time it had been an instrument of protection, as Moses used it to chase away any predators of the sheep. It had been an instrument of rescue, as Moses used it's crook to extricate lambs from the tight places they had wandered into. It had been an instrument of strength, as Moses leaned on it to steady himself after many hours of work. It had been a symbol of his calling, as Moses carried it leaning on his shoulder as an outward reminder to all that saw him that he was a shepherd – a tender of sheep. Yes, that staff had been used for noble service for forty years – just like every other shepherd's staff had been used. But something happened that day at the burning bush that forever transformed it in the staff hall of fame. God called out to Moses and said. "What do you have there in your hand?" And when God instructed him, Moses surrendered it to God – he dropped it right there before God. And when God told him to pick it back up, from then on it became an instrument of His glory.

On your journey through the wilderness, God desires to demonstrate His presence and His power through your life each and every step of the way. He desires to part the seas that obstruct you, draw out the waters that will satisfy you and defeat the enemies that oppose you. He has permitted you to encounter each and every one of those obstacles so that He might manifest His power through your life so that a watching world might see His power working on your behalf for His glory. You've heard the saying, "In God's hands, any old staff will do." Well that's right. It's not about the staff. It's not about the one who is carrying it. It's about the One to whom they have been surrendered. God desires to bring honor to His name through His children. He desires to use your talents and possessions – those things in your hand – for that same purpose. It wasn't by coincidence that Moses came to the bush that day with staff in hand. God had already provided it many years before for His divine purpose – a purpose that became clearer that day at the bush when God called Moses to that wilderness journey. When God called him to the journey, He called his person and his possessions.

Take whatever it is that God has placed in your hands and renew your commitment to Him – not only of your person, but also of your talents and possessions. Allow Him to take them and use them to manifest His presence and His power though your life in a way that only He can – a way that brings glory to Him before all people. That's why He gave them to you to begin with. They were a part of His provision for the journey. And in His hands – yes, any old staff will do!

* * *

20

YOU'RE NOT ALONE, IT'S A FAMILY AFFAIR

While the people of Israel were still at Rephidim, the warriors of Amalek came to fight against them. Moses commanded Joshua, "Call the Israelites to arms, and fight the army of Amalek. Tomorrow, I will stand at the top of the hill with the staff of God in my hand."
So Joshua did what Moses had commanded. He led his men out to fight the army of Amalek. Meanwhile Moses, Aaron, and Hur went to the top of a nearby hill. As long as Moses held up the staff with his hands, the Israelites had the advantage. But whenever he lowered his hands, the Amalekites gained the upper hand. Moses' arms finally became too tired to hold up the staff any longer. So Aaron and Hur found a stone for him to sit on. Then they stood on each side, holding up his hands until sunset. As a result, Joshua and his troops were able to crush the army of Amalek.
Exodus 17:8-13

* * *

The Israelites were, as you remember, descendants of Jacob (the grandson of Abraham), whom God had renamed Israel after they wrestled by the Jabbok brook (Gen 32:28). The Amalekites were the descendants of Amalek, the grandson of Esau (the brother of Israel and the grandson of Abraham). It had been approximately 440 years since the families of Esau and Israel had met. During the ensuing years, while the descendants of Israel had been enslaved in Egypt, the descendants of Esau (the Amalekites) had established their territory in the southern part of the land promised to Abraham, and through him to Isaac, and through him to

Israel. Remember Esau had given up that birthright (Gen 25:33); he had been despoiled of his blessing (Gen 27:36-37). The land that the Amalekites now inhabited was in fact the birthright of their "cousins", the Israelites. But these were not "kissing cousins". The Amalekites knew all too well about the birthright they had lost. They knew that the Israelites intended to occupy that land. And they were determined to retain through battle that which they had already lost many years earlier through birthright. The warriors of the Amalekite branch of the family tree had come to defeat and destroy their Israelite cousins. So Moses commanded Joshua to call the Israelites to arms to fight the army of Amalek.

Then Moses called Aaron and Hur to go to the top of a hill that over-looked the field of battle – the field where the descendants of Abraham – Israelite and Amalekite – would battle with one another. It was appro-priate that Moses should ask Aaron and Hur to join him. Aaron was of course the older brother of Moses, whom God had ordained to be Moses' spokesperson. But what you may not know is that Hur was Moses' brother-in-law. The historian Josephus tells us that Hur was the husband of Moses' sister Miriam. We will later see Hur assigned another position of leadership, as well as the assignment given to Hur's grandson (Moses' great nephew) Bezalel to construct the tabernacle. (But, forgive me; again i am getting ahead of myself.)

God had led Moses to stand at the top of the hill with the staff of God in his hand; and God had promised that as long as the staff remained upraised the Israelite branch of the family – God's chosen people – would have the advantage. God didn't promise them that they would not have to fight their cousins; rather, He assured them of victory if they followed His instruction. But it wouldn't be accomplished through any one person indi-vidually. No, it would involve the whole family. God had surrounded Moses specifically, as well as the people, with family through whom He desired to equip him, and them, for His purpose. God knew Moses could not keep his hands upraised by himself and he provided brothers to stand on either side to hold up his hands until the task was completed. God knew that Joshua could not defeat the army of Amalek by himself and he provided an army of brothers to fight along side of him.

i am mindful that God does not intend our journey through the wilder-ness to be a solo event. God has raised up family members – both family by birth, as well as family by rebirth – to walk with us, to hold up our arms, to fight along side of us, and to encourage us in the journey. Never think for one moment that God has sent you out all alone. Yes, it is He who is leading you and it is He who is strengthening you – but watch for the family that He brings along side of you to accomplish His purpose. And never think that this journey is just about you – it's God's journey – and He intends it to be a family affair.

* * *

21

THE UNDERSTUDY

While the people of Israel were still at Rephidim, the warriors of Amalek came to fight against them. Moses commanded Joshua, "Call the Israelites to arms, and fight the army of Amalek. Tomorrow, I will stand at the top of the hill with the staff of God in my hand."
So Joshua did what Moses had commanded. He led his men out to fight the army of Amalek. Meanwhile Moses, Aaron, and Hur went to the top of a nearby hill. As long as Moses held up the staff with his hands, the Israelites had the advantage. But whenever he lowered his hands, the Amalekites gained the upper hand. Moses' arms finally became too tired to hold up the staff any longer. So Aaron and Hur found a stone for him to sit on. Then they stood on each side, holding up his hands until sunset. As a result, Joshua and his troops were able to crush the army of Amalek.
Exodus 17:8-13

* * *

This is the earliest reference that we see in Scripture to Joshua. Up to this point, he's been that quiet understudy, lost in the sea of faces in the crowd. We're not told about his life in the Egyptian slave camps, nor about any key role he might have played at the crossing of the Red Sea. We don't know where he was standing a few days earlier when the people of Israel were threatening to stone Moses due to the lack of water there at Rephidim. (i personally think he was standing right at Moses' side, prepared to defend and protect him if the need arose.) But what we do know, is that God had been at work in his life, long before he became visible to us onlookers.

It takes a unique person to be an understudy. You have to be content to stand outside of the limelight. You have to be willing to work just as hard, if not harder than, the person under which you are studying. At the same time you will receive little or no recognition, affirmation, or remuneration. Let's face it; you're not getting the big bucks! You have to be prepared to step into that main role for which you have been prepared at a moment's notice; never really knowing when that moment might be. And then you have to be prepared and willing to step back into the shadows once you have completed your assigned task. You're like that racer in the gate, all set to explode out of the starting blocks, listening intently for the starting gun; and most of the time it never goes off. You must be one who is willing to be a servant to the one under whom you are studying. You must be a focused student, learning all that is possible to learn from your mentor – learning what to do AND what not to do.

It takes a unique person to properly train an understudy. You have to be willing to pour your life into someone, with the goal being that they will go farther than you have gone – they will excel beyond your limitations. You have to be willing to share the secrets that you have learned along the way – those things that have made you successful. You must also be willing to share the mistakes you have made, so that your understudy will not have to repeat them. You have to be willing to understand that as much as they are there to serve you, you are there to serve them. As they develop in their skill, you must not see them as a threat to your position but an opportunity to accomplish even greater achievements. You must be willing along the way to let them step in to exercise what they have learned; and at the appropriate time, you must be willing to step aside and let them step out into the role for which you have prepared them.

Joshua was a great understudy, which tells us that Moses was a great mentor. And here at the battle of Rephidim, Joshua steps into that role of leadership to lead the Israelites in battle. And Moses does, as God directed him, what any great mentor should do – he got off the field of battle so the Israelites knew to look to Joshua, and not Moses. Then he went up to the top of the hill so that he had a good vantage point to observe, to encourage and to be an encouragement – and most importantly, to lift up Joshua and the Israelite army before the Lord. Moses' role became one of intercession. If the staff in his hands lowered, the enemy gained the upper hand. Moses' role was paramount; he had to step aside and let his under-study take the lead so that he (Moses) would be free to do the greater work of intercession. Because Moses knew and the people saw that that is where the battle would be won!

Our Lord Jesus Christ has commissioned us to make disciples. As you journey across the wilderness, be mindful that He has placed you in the role of being somebody's understudy. Be a Joshua to your Moses. But also be mindful that He has placed you in the role of training an understudy. Be a Moses to your Joshua. And as you do both, you will see God accomplish His victory to His glory at your Rephidim.

* * *

22

HE IS YOUR BANNER

While the people of Israel were still at Rephidim, the warriors of Amalek came to fight against them. Moses commanded Joshua, "Call the Israelites to arms, and fight the army of Amalek. Tomorrow, I will stand at the top of the hill with the staff of God in my hand." ...As a result, Joshua and his troops were able to crush the army of Amalek. Then the LORD instructed Moses, "Write this down as a permanent record, and announce it to Joshua: I will blot out every trace of Amalek from under heaven." Moses built an altar there and called it "The LORD Is My Banner." He said, "They have dared to raise their fist against the LORD's throne, so now the LORD will be at war with Amalek generation after generation."
Exodus 17:8-9, 13-16

* * *

The Israelites saw the warriors of Amalek assembling for a fight there in the valley of Rephidim. The last army that had assembled against the Israelites had perished at the bottom of the Red Sea. The Israelites had not been called upon to go into battle to defeat that army. No Israelite blood had been spilled. The casualty count at that battle had been: Egyptians – ALL, Israelites – NONE. God had gone before the Israelites, making a way for their escape, and He had gone behind them, making a way for their enemy's defeat. There was no question for either army that God had fought the battle for His people that day - and He had won! Remember, God had promised that He would defeat the Egyptians so that the whole world would know that there was one God, and His Name is Jehovah! The reports of how God had gone before His people and had defeated the Egyptian army that day traveled across the land. It was heard by the Ammonites, the Moabites, the Edomites – every "ite" – including the Amalekites.

So look at the arrogance of the Amalekites. God had defeated the most powerful army in the world – the Egyptians. He had moved heaven and earth to defeat them. He had revealed His power and His glory to a watching world. He had firmly established His reputation that there was none like Him. He is the Sovereign and Almighty God, and these were His people. And here come the Amalekites advancing to fight the Israelites – but get this - shaking their fist at the Lord God Jehovah and declaring war against His throne. You see when an enemy advances against a people that God has declared to be His, that enemy is not only advancing against that people, they are advancing against His throne – and God WILL protect His throne. It wasn't so much that the Amalekites had chosen the wrong people to engage in battle, they had chosen the wrong God!

i can't help but wonder if the Israelites, as they saw the Amalekites forming their battle lines, were wondering, "How is God going to annihilate this army? We can't wait to see how He's going to do it this time. i wonder if He's going to rain down fire from heaven or bury them in the sand. i wonder if He will lead us up to the hilltop so that we can have a ringside seat like we did the last time." i tend to think they were slightly surprised when Joshua called them to arms. This wasn't how God had done it the last time. Why didn't God just wipe them out? Then they saw Moses standing on the top of the hill holding up the staff. The same staff he had when the Red Sea parted and the same staff he had stretched out when the sea came back together. But this time, Joshua was shouting, "Charge!" This time, they were face to face with the enemy in battle; and this time they were seeing the blood of friends and family spilled on the field. They saw that at one moment they were defeating the Amalekites, but at the next, they were being defeated. And they began to observe that the trend of the battle followed the position of the staff. When the staff was upraised they prevailed; God was giving His people the victory. The staff had become a symbol of their Banner of Victory. Their Banner of Victory was Jehovah Nissi ("The Lord is my Banner"). He was going before them on the battlefield. He was making the way. Though He had required them to take up the sword this time, the victory was no less His.

Are you encountering the Amalekites in your wilderness journey? Are you a child of Jehovah? Has He declared you to be His? Are you following Him in this journey? Is He the One that has begun it? Then the One that they battle is the One that they cannot defeat! His victory is assured – and He is your Banner! He may require you to take up arms, but take heart – the outcome is assured. He will give you the strength. He will guide your every effort. Keep your eye on your Banner!

And at the end of the battle, be faithful to build an altar – to testify to His faithfulness to this generation – your fellow sojourners - and all that may come behind you in the days to come.

* * *

23

A PRINCE, PAPA, AND PRIEST

Word soon reached Jethro, the priest of Midian and Moses' father-in-law, about all the wonderful things God had done for Moses and his people, the Israelites. He had heard about how the LORD had brought them safely out of Egypt. ...So Moses went out to meet his father-in-law. ...Moses told his father-in-law about everything the LORD had done to rescue Israel from Pharaoh and the Egyptians. He also told him about the problems they had faced along the way and how the LORD had delivered his people from all their troubles. "Praise be to the LORD," Jethro said, "for he has saved you from the Egyptians and from Pharaoh. He has rescued Israel from the power of Egypt! I know now that the LORD is greater than all other gods, because his people have escaped from the proud and cruel Egyptians." Then Jethro presented a burnt offering and gave sacrifices to God. As Jethro was doing this, Aaron and the leaders of Israel came out to meet him. They all joined him in a sacrificial meal in God's presence.
Exodus 18:1, 7-8, 10-12

* * *

The Midianites were descendants of Midian, the fourth son of Abraham born by his concubine Keturah. We read in Genesis 25:5 that "Abraham gave all that he had to Isaac; but to the sons of his concubines, Abraham gave gifts while he was still living, and sent them away from his son Isaac eastward, to the land of the east." Thus the descendants of Midian – the Midianites – and the descendants of Isaac and Jacob – the Israelites – were cousins. And Abraham had given the land east of the Sinai Peninsula and the Gulf of Aqaba to the Midianites. The Midianites were well known for their shrewdness in business. It was a group of Midianite tradesmen that bought Joseph from his brothers for twenty shekels of silver (Gen 37:28), and then were used by God to provide him with transportation to Egypt. There they sold him for a profit to Potiphar. This same people who were unknowingly instrumental in helping the Israelites get to Egypt were now greeting them upon their exodus from that land. Having just experienced God's victory over their cousins the Amalekites, the Israelites were about to meet the friendlier branch of the family. The Midianites had heard of God's deliverance of the Israelites from Egypt – His acts had become notorious throughout the region. And a few days earlier the Amalekites had been sent packing, so the Midianites wanted to clearly convey their warmest greetings to their Israelite cousins. So as a noble prince of the people of Midian, Jethro came to Sinai to greet the Israelites as an ambassador of goodwill.

These were more than just cousins; these were Moses' in-laws. Moses was married to Jethro's daughter Zipporah and was the father of his two grandchildren. Moses had served Jethro faithfully and had received his preparation for how to lead over a million ungrateful people through the wilderness, by tending Jethro's flocks for forty years. And Jethro, having heard how God had blessed the efforts of his son-in-law and how He had moved on behalf of His people, had a natural pride in the achievements of Moses. So as a proud papa-in-law of Moses, Jethro came to Sinai to express his pride and his affection toward Moses.

Jethro was also the priest of the people of Midian. He was their religious leader. Though He had believed in the God of Abraham; he had also believed in many gods. But Jethro could not deny that the God of Abraham, Isaac and Jacob had rescued this people from the hands of the Egyptians. God had demonstrated His presence and His power in such a way that Jethro knew that there was none like Him. So as the priest of the people of Midian, Jethro came to Sinai to prepare and present a sacrificial offering, entering into fellowship with God and His people.

But that offering was offered not only by Jethro the priest, it was offered by Jethro the person. On that day as Jethro sat down with Moses and Aaron and all the elders of Israel and ate that sacrificial meal before God, he was declaring his personal allegiance to Jehovah, the God of his son-in-law, Moses, and now his God. And on that day, He entered into God's presence and became a person of faith.

Throughout your wilderness journey you too will be greeted by princes (those in authority), papas (family members and friends) and priests (those in spiritual authority). Each will have their own reason for wanting to greet you in the midst of your journey. Some will come like Jethro - to hear firsthand what God has done, to encourage you and to affirm you in your journey, and to celebrate with you in God's victories. Others will come with different motivation, like the Amalekites - attempting to deny the activity of God, to discourage you in your pursuit, and to dissuade you from further progress in your pilgrimage. God will use those encounters to draw the "Jethro's" to Himself, and to defeat the Amalekites. In Psalm 37:23 we read, *"the steps of a good man are ordered by the Lord."* A good friend of mine once said God not only orders our steps, He also orders our stops. And in the midst of those steps and stops, He will permit us to have a reunion with princes, papas and priests. Use those reunions as an opportunity to recite and celebrate the victories you have seen along the way, and allow God to use those testimonies to transform the princes, the papas and the priests into persons of faith.

* * *

24

A MULTI-CULTURAL MESSAGE

Some time before this, Moses had sent his wife, Zipporah, and his two sons to live with Jethro, his father-in-law. The name of Moses' first son was Gershom, for Moses had said when the boy was born, "I have been a stranger in a foreign land." The name of his second son was Eliezer, for Moses had said at his birth, "The God of my fathers was my helper; he delivered me from the sword of Pharaoh." Jethro now came to visit Moses, and he brought Moses' wife and two sons with him. They arrived while Moses and the people were camped near the mountain of God. Moses was told, "Jethro, your father-in-law, has come to visit you. Your wife and your two sons are with him."
Exodus 18:2-6

* * *

M oses was "multi-cultural" before the word existed. He had been born an Israelite, raised an Egyptian, and had married a Midianite. He had been born into the priesthood of the tribe of Levi, raised as a prince in the palace of Pharaoh, and married into the royal family of Midian. He had been born as a slave, educated as a prince, "employed" as a shepherd and called by God to lead His people. Even the name of his firstborn son, Gershom, declared to the world that he lived as a stranger in a foreign land. And Gershom, having been a byproduct of that union, would forever, through the very utterance of his name, be a testimony of God's divine direction on Moses' life.

You will recall that the last time Moses had seen his wife and sons was at the inn where their second son, Eliezer, was circumcised (Exodus 4:24-26). You will also recall that God had stopped Moses while he was en route to Egypt on God's mission. Moses had allowed his multiculturalism to cloud his reasoning and had been disobedient to God, making him ill prepared to be an instrument and servant of Jehovah. You will recall the "kafuffle" that resulted between Moses and this daughter of a Midianite priest over the circumcision of their son. Moses had then proceeded on God's mission with Aaron, having sent his wife and sons to return to the home of his father-in-law. i would venture to guess that, based upon their last recorded conversation at the inn, that parting was probably not a nominee for "romantic scene of the year". As a matter of fact, i would further venture that after that crisis, which had developed due to the differences of the cultures and beliefs between Moses and Zipporah, she was thinking that if Moses didn't return, that was "okay by her". i find myself wondering what stellar thoughts and attitudes Jethro had for his son-in-law, when Zipporah and the boys ended up back on his doorstep.

But now, let's return to the reunion at Sinai. Jethro has heard the glorious reports of what God has done on the Israelites' behalf. He has heard how God has so miraculously used Moses, and now he believes that his daughter has been better matched than he ever thought or could have possibly expected. This guy was "busting out his britches" with pride for his son-in-law, as well as his own pride to be Moses' father-in-law. So he loaded up his daughter and grandchildren so that they all might be reunited post-haste. i wonder if Zipporah at this point is still the reluctant bride, or if absence truly does make the heart grow fonder, or if the news reports had changed her perspective as well. However, i don't believe the reunion between Moses and Zipporah was too heart-warming, because Moses records the kiss and embrace between he and Jethro and remains silent on that account with Zipporah!

Having just walked through the tensions of this multi-cultural relationship, why did God permit the one who He would use in such a mighty way to participate in this societal multi-cultural experiment? We can see how God used his Israelite birth and his Egyptian upbringing, but why the Midianite marriage? Remember, that God was now going global in disseminating the "story of His glory" (as Steven Hawthorne calls it). God had chosen the Israelites to be His people through whom He would reveal Himself to the entire world – Jew and Gentile. The union of Moses (Jew) and Zipporah (Gentile) was a visual example of that revelation. And Jethro's response, his acceptance of Jehovah, is indicative of the good news being received throughout the world among every tribe and tongue.

God goes on to use the descendants of Moses' sons in positions of leader-ship among the Israelites for the furtherance of His purpose.

As you travel in your wilderness journey be mindful that God has placed you, or allowed you to develop, unique relationships; both to prepare you for His purpose, and also to accomplish His purpose to spread the story of His glory. i, for one, am grateful that God did not limit salvation to one group of people; He extends it to the whole world! i would not have a relationship with Him if He had not! Allow Him to use you in those rela-tionships He has given you to accomplish His purpose!

* * *

25

I CAN'T LOVE THESE PEOPLE

Then Moses pleaded with the LORD, "What should I do with these people? They
are about to stone me!"
...The next day, Moses sat as usual to hear the people's complaints against each
other. They were lined up in front of him from morning till evening.
Exodus 17:4; 18:13

* * *

I t's true confession time — i know i couldn't do this! The Israelites were
ready to stone Moses yesterday, and today he is resolved to serve
them. Yesterday they were raging at him with anger, bitterness and anxiety, yet today, he is responding to them with peace, wisdom and patience.
Yesterday they were being used as an instrument of Satan to lash out at
him, under the burden of their sin, yet today he was being used as an
instrument of God to reach out to them, that they might be freed of the
burden of their sin. Yesterday he was the object of their wrath; today he is
being used as instrument of their deliverance.

As i read this passage, i am reminded of another account. We see Jesus,
having been whipped, stoned, mocked, and even now, being crucified,
and He sees His attackers through eyes of compassion and cries out to the
Father, "Forgive them; for they do not know what they are doing."
Blinded by their sin, they were lashing out at the one in front of them;
having lost sight that He was the only One who had the answer that
would free them of their burden. That's what sin does; it blinds us and

causes us to lose sight of the One who can free us of the burden of our sin. And yet, being without sin, Jesus could see past their sin at the need of the person.

And in the wilderness that day, Moses looked at the people with those same eyes of compassion – those same eyes that saw beyond their sin and saw their need. Moses, by himself, did not have those kind of eyes. His human eyes, like ours, couldn't see beyond the stones that were being thrown at him. His human ears, like ours, couldn't hear over the grumblings, complaints and threats of the crowd. Even his human heart, like ours, couldn't love in the face of the hatred that was being expressed by the crowd. And yet, he saw, he heard, and he responded with those kind of eyes, ears, and heart.

Now, you and i understand that Jesus was able to respond like that, but He's God. The bigger question is - how was Moses able to respond with that kind of love, patience and compassion? Even closer to home, how could you and i possibly respond to others in that way? i mean, sure, Jesus said the second greatest commandment is to love others as we do ourselves – i understand that is the standard – but how can i possibly achieve it? The Good News is that Jesus didn't just set the standard and walk away; if i am a follower of Jesus He enables me to walk in His way. God's standard for Moses was that no matter what the people might do, he was compelled to love them. But even more importantly, God's solution for Moses was that through His Spirit, he was enabled to love them. Moses was no longer seeing the people through his eyes, he was seeing them through God's eyes. He wasn't hearing them through his ears, but through God's. He wasn't responding to them with his human heart, he was responding through the heart of God.

Our Lord has given us His Spirit that we might not only "will" to walk according to His good purpose, but as Paul writes that we might also "do" according to His good purpose. It was God's Spirit that enabled Moses to love the children of Israel; it will be God's Spirit that enables you to love those unlovely, complaining, cantankerous people that He has placed in your path of your wilderness journey. No, like i said at the beginning, i can't love them, and you can't love them, but God can love them – and does! So will you, if you will allow Him to change your heart and so that He can love them – and serve them – through you.

* * *

26

THE COMPLAINT DESK

The next day, Moses sat as usual to hear the people's complaints against each other. They were lined up in front of him from morning till evening. ...Moses replied, "Well, the people come to me to seek God's guidance. When an argument arises, I am the one who settles the case. I inform the people of God's decisions and teach them his laws and instructions."
Exodus 18:13, 15-16

* * *

W ho wants Moses' job? This morning you are scheduled to listen to the people's complaints. After a brief lunch, this afternoon you are scheduled to listen to the people's complaints. And tonight - you guessed it – after dinner, you are scheduled to listen to the people's complaints. Do you see those two words in verse 13 "as usual"? This was Moses' "usual" schedule.

The line of negative, complaining people was endless, because as soon as one complaint was resolved, the people would find they had another complaint, and they'd get back in line. And the "wonderful" thing for the people was that Moses had set up a complaint desk. All of us like a complaint desk – a place where we can go to vent our complaints and make them someone else's problem to fix. i have a complaint and you're supposed to solve it. That's how it works! And Moses had established himself as the Grand Umpire of Fighting and Frustration ("GUFF"). At this rate, they were complaining longer and faster than they were walking – and they were doing exactly what they were being led by Moses to do! Moses had established himself to be the one who settled each complaint. He had determined that only he could hear from God and therefore he must be the one to inform the people of God's decision and instruction. He would take every burden on himself. Moses was a "co-dependent" before the term existed – Moses needed to be needed, and the people had no difficulty meeting that need.

Paul wrote to the early church, *"Bear ye one another's burdens, and thus fulfill the law of Christ"* (Gal 6:2 KJV). Then three verses later he wrote, *"For every man shall bear his own burden"* (Gal 6:5 KJV). Wait a minute, we're to bear one another's burdens, but we are to bear our own burden? Was Paul contradicting himself? No. In verse 2, the word he uses for "burdens" is "baros" – meaning "a weight that is burdensome or heavy" – a weight that is beyond what any one person bear alone. Whereas in verse 5, the word he uses for "burden" is "phortion" – meaning "something that is to be carried" – a weight that is for each person to bear alone. And Jesus taught *"Come to Me, all of you who are weary and carry heavy burdens, and I will give you rest. Take My yoke upon you. Let Me teach you, because I am humble and gentle, and you will find rest for your souls. For My yoke fits perfectly, and the burden I give you is light"* (Matt 11:28-30).

What can we learn from the lesson of the complaint desk and how can we apply it to our lives? First, as a follower of Jesus, He has told us to bring every burden, every complaint and every trial to Him and that He will exchange it for His burden, and the burden He gives us will be light, for the weight of sin will have been removed from it – our sin-filled burden will have been exchanged for a sin-less burden. Second, there will be burdens – trials – that God permits us, as His children, to experience that are not intended for us to carry alone. We are to share those burdens with others that are journeying with us so that together we might bear that burden. God has uniquely selected and shaped our fellow sojourners for just that purpose of bearing together that burden. But we are to be discerning, and not attempt to carry that burden that was intended to be born by one's self. Third, do not make the mistake that Moses made of putting yourself in the position of having people look to you instead of looking to the Lord. He is the only one who can exchange our sin-filled burden for His sin-less burden. We must continually point others to Him. And if we will shutdown the complaint desk and release the complaints to God, He will take those complaints and transform them into blessings; He will take the time we otherwise would have wasted and use it to further His purpose; and He will transform us from complainers to encouragers as we continue in the journey.

* * *

27

A FEW GOOD MEN (AND WOMEN)

*When Moses' father-in-law saw all that Moses was doing for the people, he said,
"Why are you trying to do all this alone? The people have been standing here all
day to get your help. This is not good!" his father-in-law exclaimed. "You're
going to wear yourself out -- and the people, too. This job is too heavy a burden
for you to handle all by yourself. Now let me give you a word of advice, and may
God be with you. ...Find some capable, honest men who fear God and hate bribes.
Appoint them as judges over groups.... ...They will help you carry the load,
making the task easier for you. If you follow this advice, and if God directs you to
do so, then you will be able to endure the pressures, and all these people will go
home in peace." Moses listened to his father-in-law's advice and followed his
suggestions.*
Exodus 18:14, 17-19, 21-24

* * *

God's plan has never been for us to be "Lone Rangers" of the faith.
God's plan has always been one of multiplying His work through
His people. Does God "need" us to spread the Gospel? Does He "need" us
to accomplish His will? No, He's God; He can accomplish it in the twinkle
of an eye using whatever means He chooses. But God chose to use His
creation – and specifically His children – to be His ambassadors in
proclaiming His Word, accomplishing His will and performing His work.
God has followed a pattern of giving away ministry since His creation of
Adam – He gave Adam dominion over His creation, and we see that
pattern continued throughout all of Scripture including the way Jesus
discipled His apostles.

Moses was breaking that principle of giving away ministry. He was having all of the people come to him for help. It was more than God ever intended for one person. And Jethro rightly told him that the violation of this principle of ministry would:

- affect Moses' health – that truly he would wear himself out,
- undermine God's plan of administering justice to the people and cause them to weary in the process, and
- prevent God's people from experiencing firsthand what He desired to do in and through their lives.

Jethro counseled Moses that he must choose leaders who would help carry the load – that it wasn't enough to be useful himself, but he must help others become useful in the administration of God's work. A credit to Moses' character is that though this counsel came from a spiritual babe, he heeded the counsel, knowing that it aligned with God's word and God's plan. Though He was the leader of this people, he was "not too wise" to receive counsel; and in so doing demonstrated great wisdom. Also, Moses demonstrated the wisdom and understanding to realize that God had already placed within that body all the human resources that were required to fulfill His work. God had already placed gifted and godly leaders in place to meet the ministry need.

Paul instructed Timothy to entrust to others those things that had been entrusted to him, that they in turn might entrust others. It is to be a continuing process. Accordingly, Jethro wisely counseled Moses in the characteristics he must be seeking in those leaders. They must be capable – don't just pick anyone, pick those who are gifted to do the job. They must be honest – they must demonstrate high integrity and be above reproach. They must be of the very best character. They must be strong and resolute in their faith and their fear of God – that they not be daunted by the frowns and complaints of the crowd, or the temptations to injustice of the world. They must understand their accountability before God. They must be unswerving in their integrity – one whose word may be taken and whose fidelity can be relied upon. And they must despise gain at the expense of others.

As you continue in your wilderness journey, whom has God surrounded you with to entrust all that He is teaching you? Does your life demonstrate the character and the qualities that would have qualified you to be one of Moses' leaders? Are you operating under the principle of giving away ministry? Are you looking for a few good men and women to disciple and entrust? God has placed them in your path. Look for them. Allow God to use you to equip them.

* * *

28

WHO IS YOUR JETHRO?

Soon after this, Moses said good-bye to his father-in-law, who returned to his own land.
Exodus 18:27

* * *

To the best of our knowledge, this is the last time Moses saw Jethro on this earth. As Jethro said good-bye to his son-in-law, he did so as a man whose life had been transformed in that wilderness valley. As he returned to the land from whence he had come, he did not return as the same man who had arrived in that valley.

Jethro was a good, kind and considerate man when he arrived in that wilderness valley. He was the father of seven daughters (you have to be good, kind and considerate if you have seven daughters!), the oldest of whom was Zipporah. One day while Zipporah and her sisters were watering their father's flock, as was often the case a group of shepherds came and threatened to drive them away from the well. But that day, an Egyptian fugitive by the name of Moses defended the women and even helped them water the flock. Jethro was grateful to this stranger. He opened his home to Moses and treated him like a son. Eventually Jethro gave Zipporah to Moses in marriage. And Moses and Zipporah gave him two grandsons. (Finally he was getting male descendants!) Moses faithfully served his father-in-law for almost forty years until God redirected his steps that day at the burning bush. Jethro graciously released Moses to

go do what he knew God had called him to do. Jethro didn't argue with
Moses. He didn't try to prevent Moses from going. He supported his son-
in-law in the decision he had made. Even when Moses decided that
Zipporah and the boys could not travel with him to Egypt, and sent them
back to Jethro's house, Jethro supported his son-in-law and took them in.

Jethro was a deeply religious man when he arrived in that wilderness
valley. Jethro, as we've already seen, was the priest of the Midianites. He
led the Midianites in religious worship of their many gods. He directed
them in their sacrifices, their religious festivals, and all of their religious
practices. Though they had heard of the God of their ancestor Abraham,
they worshipped Him among many. (Truly then they did not worship
Him, because the Lord God Jehovah is not one among many and He alone
is worthy of worship.)

Jethro was a man of wise judgment when he arrived in that wilderness
valley. Jethro, as we have also seen, was a prince of the Midianites. He was
a leader among their governing council. He demonstrated wise judgment
by coming to greet the Israelites as an ambassador of peace. He gave
Moses wise counsel in how to delegate authority so as to more efficiently
settle the Israelites' disputes. In Proverbs 28:23 we read, "*In the end, people
appreciate frankness more than flattery.*" Moses received his father-in-law's
frankness because Jethro had consistently demonstrated wise judgment.

But no matter how good, or how kind, or how religious or how wise
Jethro was, that day when he arrived in the wilderness valley, he was a
spiritually lost man. Just as many in our day, he was a man who knew
about God, but did not know God. But just as God was ordering the steps
of Moses and the Israelites, so had He ordered the steps of Jethro. Yes, He
used Jethro to bring Zipporah and the boys back to Moses. Yes, He used
Jethro to give Moses wise counsel. But most importantly, He allowed
Jethro to hear firsthand from his son-in-law about the goodness and the
glory of the Lord God Jehovah. As Moses gave an account of God's presence, power and provision throughout the journey, Jethro for the first time
came to see the Person of God and the relationship that existed between
He and His people. And Jethro realized that for all of his religious activity,
he did not have that relationship – and his heart hungered for it! That day,
when Jethro led the children of God in worship of the One True God,
Jethro became a man who knew God, and became a man whom God
could use.

Through his experience in that wilderness valley, Jethro became a man with a heart to seek and to serve God and a man who God did use. Later in Judges 1:16 we see the descendants of Jethro, the Kenites, fighting along side of and settling with the tribe of Judah in the Promised Land. The Kenites were a people who followed and served God because they were pointed to Him by an ancestor (Jethro) who loved Him, knew Him, served Him and reflected Him in his life.

Jethro's was a life that God transformed in the wilderness through the faithful obedience and testimony of His people. Remember as you journey, that **the wilderness is not the process that will lead you to God's purpose for your life; the wilderness is a <u>part</u> of God's purpose for your life**. Don't get so focused on the destination that you lose sight of what He is doing in and through your life right now. Don't miss the people He brings to you – including those family members – who only know about Him, but do not know Him. God's whole purpose for your journey might be that He raises up a Kenite people who follow Him as a result of your faithfulness and obedience with this one. Look around. Who is your Jethro?

* * *

29

GOD, YOU LEFT OUT A FEW DETAILS

*Then God told him, "I will be with you. And this will serve as proof that I have
sent you: When you have brought the Israelites out of Egypt, you will return here
to worship God at this very mountain."*
*…The Israelites arrived in the wilderness of Sinai exactly two months after they
left Egypt. After breaking camp at Rephidim, they came to the base of Mount
Sinai and set up camp there. Then Moses climbed the mountain to appear
before God.*
Exodus 3:12; 19:1-3

* * *

God promised Moses that day at the burning bush that after he had
brought the children of Israel out of Egypt, he would return to that
mountain to worship God. It had been months since God had given him
that promise. He had suffered rejection by His wife when the journey
began. He had suffered ridicule by the Egyptians when he delivered God's
message. He had suffered rebellion by the Israelites almost every step of
the way. He had been subjected to more grumbling, complaints and death
threats than anyone before or anyone since has had to endure. And none
of those were a part of God's promise. God had not said, "After you have
been the object of rejection, ridicule and rebellion, you will return here and
worship Me." God had said, "After you've completed the assignment I've
given you, you will return here and worship Me."

God didn't tell Moses all that he was going to encounter along the way.

God knew Moses' frame; and He knew that if Moses knew everything that was going to unfold, Moses would never step out on the journey. He would have determined to stay right there at the burning bush. i mean, "God, if You're going to bring me right back here to worship You, let's just skip all the stuff in the middle. i want to get right to the good stuff at the end of the journey." Or even if Moses had stepped out to begin the journey, he would be plotting, planning and contriving how to overcome each of these obstacles on his own. For example, if Moses had known that the Egyptian army was going to attack at the Red Sea, he could have led the Israelites another way – through the land of the Philistines (Ex 13:17). Or if Moses had known that there would be no water at Rephidim (Ex 17:2), he could have had the Israelites make preparations for extra provision of water before they left the sweet springs of Elim. There are many things that Moses could have done differently if God had let him know what was going to unfold. But God chose not to. And instead of going around the Red Sea, they went through the Red Sea. Instead of carrying sweet water, they tasted the sweet water that gushed out of the rock. Instead of Moses being commended for his wisdom and foresight, God moved in the miraculous way that only God can move – and He alone got the glory.

The key truth we must grasp here is that **though God did not reveal ahead of time all of the steps that would lead to His promise, His promise assured that He would lead through those steps**. God's promise always assures us that He will lead though every circumstance we encounter to accomplish His purpose, fulfilling His promise. His promise assures that we will lack for no provision for the fulfilling of His promise. Yes, we will probably encounter rejection, ridicule and rebellion. We will certainly encounter obstacles and circumstances that are beyond our ability to overcome. We will find ourselves in situations that will cause us to look back and second-guess some of our decisions. But learn from Moses. God has permitted you to encounter that obstacle, circumstance or situation in the midst of the journey to His promise because He desires to use it to magnify His Name – to accomplish what only He can! God is jealous for His glory. He will not share it with anyone or anything. And He desires – He has set you on this journey – that His Name might be further glorified. Heed His promise and commit the circumstances to Him!

But there is one more thing we must see here. The Moses that has returned to the mountain to worship God is not the Moses that stood before the burning bush. Throughout these months of rejection, ridicule and rebellion, there has been no one for Moses to turn to except his Lord. As a result, Moses has experienced an intimacy – a closeness – that can only come through the trials. It is the experiences in the valley that prepare us for the worship on the mountain. Yes, don't misunderstand me; we must worship our Lord in the valley as well. We must worship Him throughout the journey, because He is worthy of our worship. But i believe, that it is while we are in the valley that we come to better understand why He is worthy of our worship. We come to better understand Who He is. In the valley when we have come to the end of ourselves – to the end of our abilities and our resources – it is there that we come to know Him more and love Him more. Then when we come to the mountain, as He has promised, we arrive with hearts that are fully-prepared to experience Him – to worship Him – and to receive all that He intends to now reveal to us on the mountain.

Remember the promise that God gave you as you began this wilderness journey. You will come to the mountain fully prepared to experience, receive and give back to Him all that He intends.

* * *

30

THOSE FAMOUS LAST WORDS

Then Moses climbed the mountain to appear before God. The LORD called out to him from the mountain and said, "Give these instructions to the descendants of Jacob, the people of Israel: You have seen what I did to the Egyptians. You know how I brought you to myself and carried you on eagle's wings. Now if you will obey me and keep my covenant, you will be my own special treasure from among all the nations of the earth; for all the earth belongs to me. And you will be to me a kingdom of priests, my holy nation.' Give this message to the Israelites." Moses returned from the mountain and called together the leaders of the people and told them what the LORD had said. They all responded together, "We will certainly do everything the LORD asks of us."
Exodus 19:3-8

* * *

"We will certainly do everything the Lord asks of us." Sure you will! Just like you did everything He asked during your last two months in the wilderness. Almost every time you were given the opportunity to make a choice to honor God, you blew it. And yet we say, "We will certainly do everything the Lord asks of us." Why do we say these stupid things? They, like us, will most certainly NOT do everything the Lord asks. If there is anything that is certain, it is our propensity to disobey God.

Look at the promise God has given them! He recounts His good works on their behalf throughout the journey. He has been victorious over the Egyptians. He has brought the Israelites out of Egypt and piloted them, provided for them, and protected them every step of the way. And if they will obey Him and remain in covenant with Him, they will be His special treasure among all the nations. They will be, not only His favorite, but also His favored, sons and daughters. They can be certain that they will never lack for anything. They can be certain that He will direct their every step. They can be certain that God will give them victory over every enemy. Talk about a promise! And all they need to do is obey God! All they need to do, is do what He leads them to do, what He provides for them to do, and what He enables them to do. Do you understand how little God was asking of them? The Lord God Jehovah, who was their Creator and loved them perfectly, would never direct them to do anything outside of His love. The Lord God Jehovah, who was their heavenly Father and desired His absolute best for them, would never direct them to do anything that wasn't in their best interest. The Lord God Jehovah, who was their Sovereign Almighty God and was able to move heaven and earth to accomplish His best, would never direct them to do anything that He would not enable them to accomplish. So what's the problem? Why do our lips say, "We certainly will", when our actions say, "We certainly will not." Why is something that should be so easy, so difficult? It reminds me of our infamous new year's resolutions that we voice with such strong conviction on January 1st and too often have broken by January 8th, if not sooner.

Can you imagine the grief in the Father's heart when He heard those empty words, knowing fully that in just a matter of days they would be worshiping a golden calf? It causes me to recall another time, when another son of Israel spoke boldly with conviction, "Lord, with You I am ready to go to prison and to death!" And Jesus said to him, "Peter, the cock will not crow today until you have denied three times that you know Me."

But God knew their frame, just like He knew Peter's, and just like He knows ours. He knew that their sin nature, just like ours, would always rebel against God. That's what sin is; it's rebellion against a holy God. The Israelites had it; and you and i have it. Everyone, except Jesus, who has ever walked this earth since that day in the Garden of Eden, has that sin nature. And God knew that there was absolutely nothing we could do on our own to overcome our sin nature. That's why He sent Jesus. Because, as our Creator, He loves us; as our Father, He desires His best for us; and as our Sovereign Almighty God, He is able to accomplish His best. His best is Jesus – in Him, through Him, because of Him and with Him.

God made the Israelites that promise knowing fully that they would not obey. They, like we, needed to come to that understanding that they would be ineffective, unable and lost on their own. Because the reality is, we won't turn to a Savior until we recognize our need for a Savior.

You and i have the privilege and the blessing today that the Israelites did not have. Jesus had not yet come to earth; He had not yet paid the price on that cross for their sin; He had not yet risen from the grave that they might walk in victorious life. You and i have that privilege. God has given us the blessing of knowing His Best, and if we will receive His Best, we are guaranteed His Best. And because Jesus has ascended to sit at the right hand of His Father, He has sent the Holy Spirit to indwell within us, to enable us to walk in His Best.

As you journey in your wilderness, are you attempting to do everything on your own? Or have you said "yes" to God's Best – Jesus. When it's all said and done, that will be the only word that matters, because then we will be able to say, together with the apostle Paul, *"I can do all things through Christ who gives me strength."*

* * *

31

THEY WILL HAVE CONFIDENCE IN YOU

Then the LORD said to Moses, "I am going to come to you in a thick cloud so the people themselves can hear me as I speak to you. Then they will always have confidence in you."
Exodus 19:9

* * *

For years an investment brokerage firm has used the slogan, "When so-and-so speaks, everybody listens." The advertisements invariably center on large groups of people in public places, going about their usual activities. But when the name of the firm is invoked, everyone stops in their tracks, and turns an ear so that they might hear the wisdom that is about to be shared. In addition to being catchy, the advertisements communicate that the firm has a proven track record of success, and its clients can also be assured of that success if they heed the firm's counsel. It infers that what they have to say is second to none. Not only can clients be confident in the message and the ones who invoke it, but also because of who has invoked it, they can have confidence in the messenger.

We, as people, hunger for truth. Our Creator endowed us with the capacity to seek truth, understand it and the need to know it. From the first day in the Garden of Eden, God has sought to meet that need by communicating His truth to His creation. God has sought out His creation that we might know Him and in knowing Him, know the essence of Who

He is – truth. Jesus Himself said, *"If you hold to My teaching… you will know the truth, and the truth will set you free"* (John 8:31-32 NIV).

God was preparing to speak His truth to Moses, and through Moses to the people. God wanted it to be very clear that it was He who was speaking, and therefore it would be His truth. The people had become accustomed to God's presence going before them in the form of a pillar of cloud ever since they had left Egypt. For two months, God led them as a pillar of cloud, and now that pillar of cloud was about to cover the peak of Mount Sinai. Months before, when God had met Moses at that place, He had used a burning bush to signify His presence to Moses. Now He intended to use a covering of cloud to signify His presence to all of the children of Israel. On neither occasion did He want there to be any confusion as to His presence, for He was about to reveal His will - His words of truth.

God was about to do two things. First, He was about to give His Ten Commandments to Moses to give to the people. These were words of life - words that spoke to God's love for them and their covenant with Him. Second, God wanted His people to know that Moses was His servant. He wanted them to know that when Moses spoke, he was speaking the words of God. He wanted the people to fully understand that He – God – had placed Moses in the role as their undershepherd. That if any difficulty was to arise between Moses and the people, the people were to take it up with God. Now a fair question to ask might be, "Since the people had been following Moses' instruction for over two months, didn't they already understand that He was God's servant?" Perhaps. But do you remember, there in the valley at Rephidim, when the people quarreled with and threatened to stone Moses? God had blessed them that day, despite their disobedience, by granting them the water that gushed from the rock. But now God was going to deal with unfinished business. God wanted them to know His word, His voice and His servant; and to clearly understand that if they were going to be His people, they must heed His word, hear His voice, and honor His servant.

We live in a world that desperately needs to hear and know the voice of God. There is a cacophony today of voices claiming to be truth, claiming to be the voice of God, or claiming to be the servant of God. But there is only one true God. And He makes His presence known. He makes His truth known. And when He speaks, He makes His servants known. As you travel on your journey through the wilderness, God desires to make His presence known in your life. If you will surrender your life to Him, releasing all control and authority to Him, He will make His presence in you obvious, His voice through you conspicuous, and His confidence in you contagious. Never lose sight that He has placed you on this journey so that He might make a global impact through your life. Therefore you can, and must, speak boldly and confidently, because of the One who speaks through you. For when God speaks, everybody listens!

* * *

32

PREPARE TO WORSHIP

Then the LORD said to Moses, "I am going to come to you in a thick cloud so the people themselves can hear me as I speak to you." ...Then the LORD told Moses, "Go down and prepare the people for my visit. Purify them today and tomorrow, and have them wash their clothing. Be sure they are ready on the third day, for I will come down upon Mount Sinai as all the people watch.
Exodus 19:9-11

* * *

We live in a day and time when worship has been watered down to its least common denominator. We use the word "worship" as a noun to refer to a weekly gathering in our churches. We use it as a verb to refer specifically to our musical expression in a church service. We use it as an adjective to refer to a specific style of music. And though, all of these in some respect are an appropriate use of the word, i do not believe that any of these begin to touch the heart of what God intends to be worship.

God told Moses, *"I am going to come to... speak to you. Go down and prepare the people for My visit."* God was about to visit His presence and His Person upon His people. They would hear His voice and they would see and experience His presence. Just as God had told Moses on that same mount months before, that ground was about to become holy ground because of the presence of the Lord God Jehovah. And worship would be the response of God's people entering into God's presence and experiencing His Person.

But before they could enter into that holy place where worship would result, they had to prepare themselves. God told them that they could not enter into His presence the way they were. They must be prepared and they must be purified. God was very specific in His instruction. Preparation to enter into His presence was so important to Him that He left nothing for the Israelites to take for granted.

First, God told Moses that the people must be purified (or sanctified). They must be set apart or cleansed from all of the business, cares and concerns of this world. In order to hear what was on the heart of God, they must be cleansed of all impure affections and disquieting passions. God knew that a five-minute prayer prior to entering into His presence was not going to prepare their hearts. He instructed them to take two days to do nothing but prepare for entering into His presence, such that everything else might be dismissed from their hearts and their minds so that there would be nothing to distract them from Him.

Second, God told them to wash their clothing – not because He is a respecter of garments, but because He desired that they prepare their whole person. As the Lord reminded Samuel, we look at the outside, while God looks at the inside. i am mindful that all too often we spend all of our time dressing up the outside and never touch the inside as we prepare for worship. If worship is my response to Who God is, it is a response that requires all of my person – physically, emotionally, intellectually and spiritually. i must then be prepared and cleansed in every respect.

Third, God told them to anticipate His arrival on the third day. i am convinced that some of us never expect to encounter God when we go to a worship service, and if we did, we would not know Him because we were not expecting Him. God clearly desired them to have an expectancy that would lead to a heightened awareness of His presence and His voice.

As you journey in the wilderness, God desires to visit you with His presence and He desires for you to hear His voice. Though we are cleansed and able to enter into His presence only through the shed blood of His Son, we must still enter into His presence with hearts that are prepared to encounter Him, hearts that are singularly focused on Him, and hearts that are attuned to Him. As we do, our response to Him will be worship – worship like John describes in the Revelation – worship that is without ritual, worship that is without routine, and worship that is without end. It will be the response of a sinner saved by the unmerited grace of a Holy God to His goodness, His grace, His mercy and His love. Prepare to worship!

* * *

33

BOUNDARIES THAT PROTECT

*Then the LORD told Moses, "Go down and prepare the people for my visit.
Purify them today and tomorrow, and have them wash their clothing. Be sure they
are ready on the third day, for I will come down upon Mount Sinai as all the
people watch. Set boundary lines that the people may not pass. Warn them, 'Be
careful! Do not go up on the mountain or even touch its boundaries. Those who
do will certainly die! Any people or animals that cross the boundary must be
stoned to death or shot with arrows. They must not be touched by human hands.'
The people must stay away from the mountain until they hear one long blast from
the ram's horn. Then they must gather at the foot of the mountain."*
Exodus 19:10-13

* * *

God was preparing to meet with His people; and He was preparing
His people to meet with Him. As we have already seen, God's
instruction to His children was very specific. If He was going to visit His
people, they needed to make preparations for Him to do so. They could
not come just as they were. Time and again, we have been reminded, as
Henry Blackaby says, "You cannot stay where you are and go with God."
The same principle holds true here: you cannot stay as you are and go
with God. This entire journey is about the preparations and adjustments
that He is making, and calling you to make, in your life in order for you to
be that *"vessel useful for the Master"* (2 Tim 2:21). Now does that mean i stay
on the sidelines until all of that preparation is done? No! Though God is
continually at work preparing us for what He is preparing for us; by His
grace He is working in us and through us right where we are. Never let

your sense of inability or your sense of inadequacy keep you from being immediately obedient (is there any other kind of obedience?) to our Lord in what He has placed before you. It is in our weakness that He is made strong; in our inadequacy where we rely on Him more; and in our inability where we see Him do what only He can. But understand, He loves you too much to leave you as you are and where you are, and He is constantly molding and shaping you.

Paul clearly describes this process in his letter to the church in Rome, *"Give your bodies to God. Let them be a living and holy sacrifice--the kind He will accept. When you think of what He has done for you, is this too much to ask? Don't copy the behavior and customs of this world, but let God transform you into a new person by changing the way you think. Then you will know what God wants you to do, and you will know how good and pleasing and perfect His will really is"* (Rom 12:1-2). That surrender and adjustment to God is an act of worship on our part, and His transformation of our lives is an act of love on His part.

God's preparation of our lives includes boundaries that He has established for our lives; boundaries that protect, not imprison. God intended to visit His people. They would hear His voice and they would witness His presence. But He was setting a boundary line beyond which they could not pass. They were not even allowed to touch the boundaries, for if they did they would die. He knew that if the people saw His face they would die, so He established the boundary to define the "safe zone" so that they could experience His presence. As their loving Heavenly Father, God set a boundary for His children.

God has set a boundary for us – a boundary within which we will experience the blessing of His presence. And He knows that the areas outside of those boundaries will lead to our death – either physically or spiritually or both. Therefore because of His love for us He has established those boundaries. i am reminded of when my children were toddlers. We had a pet dog, Ezekiel, that became a part of our family long before the birth of our children. Ezekiel did not appreciate the intrusion of the children into the family, let alone his "dining area". Violations into that area by either of the children were met with loud barking and growling. i can still see their "sweet, angelic faces" looking up at us as they tried to cross the boundary out of the safe zone. And they can still to this day show you the scar from the bite they received from Ezekiel for their efforts. The unfortunate reality is that we, like them, want to continually "test' the boundaries. We want to walk up to them and touch them, or see what happens when we take one step over them. We act as if God is a "cosmic killjoy" who just wants us to miss out on something good. Or perhaps, it's just the temptation of forbidden fruit. Whatever our motive or our motivation, we step across that line, and whatever was waiting for us on the other side of that boundary sinks its teeth into us. And either it drags us further and further into the area that we shouldn't have entered, to the point that we can no longer find our way back; or at the very minimum we are scarred for life.

Each of us has a testimony of how God by His grace has rescued us from the mire when we have crossed over His boundary into forbidden territory. But fellow travelers let us not presume on His grace. God has set His boundaries around our path as we journey through this wilderness. Heed those boundaries; they are boundaries that protect!

* * *

34

WHEN GOD SHOWS UP, YOU KNOW IT

On the morning of the third day, there was a powerful thunder and lightning storm, and a dense cloud came down upon the mountain. There was a long, loud blast from a ram's horn, and all the people trembled. Moses led them out from the camp to meet with God, and they stood at the foot of the mountain. All Mount Sinai was covered with smoke because the LORD had descended on it in the form of fire. The smoke billowed into the sky like smoke from a furnace, and the whole mountain shook with a violent earthquake. As the horn blast grew louder and louder, Moses spoke, and God thundered his reply for all to hear. The LORD came down on the top of Mount Sinai and called Moses to the top of the mountain. So Moses climbed the mountain.
Exodus 19:16-20

* * *

Prophecy indicates that on the Sunday after Christ returns to rapture His saints, there will be "professing Christians" who still gather in church buildings across the world for a meeting that will have everything to do with ritual and nothing to do with a relationship with the Father through Jesus Christ. The unfortunate reality in many of our evangelical churches even today is that God's presence is absent and nobody is noticing. We have become so accustomed to running through an "order of worship" that we haven't even noticed that the One whom we came to worship is nowhere around because we have become satisfied to gather without Him. But the absence of His presence is not only apparent in our church services, His absence is apparent in our lives.

His absence is conspicuous in our prayer lives, as we issue meaningless repetitions before we eat or sleep. i once attended a worship service where one of the men was asked to pray an offertory prayer. He proceeded to pray, "And God thank you for this food which we are about to eat." This man was so programmed to say those words when he prayed; he didn't even notice that the plate that was about to be passed wasn't the meat platter! We issue these repetitions without any regard for God; totally missing the fact that prayer is conversing with the Lord God Jehovah, the Creator and Sovereign God of the universe. We have been given the privilege and ability to enter into His presence through the shed blood of His Son, Who is sitting at the Father's right hand, giving us access to His very ear! And yet we ramble on with meaningless platitudes as if our voice will not be heard above the ceiling.

His absence is conspicuous in the absence of His joy in our lives. Paul writes that we have great joy in the presence of God. We will not always be happy; *happiness* will be predicated on what is *happening* in our lives, but His joy will endure regardless of our circumstances. As the psalmist writes, "*God is the source of all my joy*" (Psa 43:4).

His absence is conspicuous in the absence of His power working through our lives. God is at work to draw a lost world unto Himself that every people, every tongue, every nation might have the opportunity to turn to Him, worship Him and bring glory to Him. And He will use every resource at His disposal; the same power that raised Jesus from the dead (Eph 1:19-20). If we are not experiencing that same resurrection power then we are not experiencing Him.

That day at Sinai, there was no question as to His presence. God made His presence known through the thunder and lightening, the cloud, the ram's horn, the fire, the smoke and the earthquake. The people could see, hear, smell, taste and feel that God was there. He left nothing to their imagination. He left no doubt as to His presence. And the people trembled in reverence and awe!

God desires to make His presence that conspicuous in and through our lives to a watching world. He desires that we walk with Him in the reverent awareness of His presence and His power. He desires to bring glory to His Name through our lives – not our glory, His! Therefore not our presence and power, but His! And where He is, He will be seen, heard, smelled, tasted and felt. Those around us will know that they have come into His presence. Moses disappeared in the cloud, and so will we – we will not be seen, He will!

Do you desire to walk in His presence? Do you desire His presence to be that conspicuous in your life? Have you invited Him to make His presence known in and through your life? Is there unconfessed sin in your life that is preventing you from walking in His presence? Are you asking Him to bring you to the end of yourself, your plans and your agenda, that you might be available to Him? He has brought you on this journey so that you might experience His presence and His power in ways that you never have before. Will you let Him?

When God shows up, you will know it – and so will those around you!

* * *

35

THERE IS NONE LIKE HIM

*Then God instructed the people as follows: "I am the LORD your God, who
rescued you from slavery in Egypt. Do not worship any other gods besides Me."*
Exodus 20:1-3

* * *

People of Israel, in case you are having difficulty remembering Who I
am, I am the LORD your God! I rescued you from slavery in Egypt. I
am the One who caused Pharaoh to release you. I am the One who parted
the Red Sea so that you could pass through it to the other side. I am the
One who defeated the Egyptian army. I am the One who gave you victory
over the Amalekites. I am the One who gave you water to drink when
there was none. I am the One who has provided you with heavenly bread
every day for over a month. I am the One who has come to you in a pillar
of cloud to lead you every step of the way since you left Egypt. There is
none like Me!

And you who are traveling in the wilderness today, do you remember
Who I am? I am the LORD your God! I rescued you from the bondage of
sin. I sent My Son to pay the ransom for your release. I sent My Son to
enter the depths of Hades, defeating sin and death, so that you might be
delivered and able to walk victoriously. I am the One who has made the
way though your wilderness. I am the One who has defeated your
enemies – Satan, the world, your flesh, and sin – through the shed blood
of My Son. I have paid the price. I am the One who has given you Living

Water so that you will never thirst. I am the One who has given you the Bread of Life so that you will never hunger. I am the One who has sent My Holy Spirit to indwell you and lead you every step of your journey. There is none like Me!

I created you. I formed you in your mother's womb. I knew you before the beginning of time. I am your Refuge and your Strength. I am your Shield and your Buckler. I am your Fortress and your Rock. I am your Banner and your Provider. I am your Courage and your Hope. I am your Deliverer and your Defender. I am your Creator and your Sustainer. I am your Rescuer and your Sanctuary. I am your Guide and your Security. I am your Good Shepherd and your Heavenly Father. I am the Sovereign and Almighty God. There is none like Me!

I have pardoned your iniquities. I have healed your diseases. I have redeemed your life from the pit. I have crowned you with lovingkindness and compassion. I have not dealt with you according to your sins, nor rewarded you according to your iniquities. I have comforted you in times of hardship. I have given you peace in times of anxiety. I have shepherded you throughout your journey. I have given you springs in your wilderness. There is none like Me!

I am the Alpha, and I am also the Omega, the Beginning and the End. I am the Giver of the Law, and I am also the Extender of Mercy. I am the Punisher of the wicked, and I am also the Rescuer of the persecuted. I am the Destroyer of the treacherous, and I am also the Defender of the defenseless. I am the Humbler of the proud, and I am also the Exalter of the humble. I am the Provider of the rich, and I am also the Provision of the poor. I am the Lord of the heavenly hosts, and I am also the King of all the earth. There is none like Me!

THEREFORE, DO NOT WORSHIP ANY OTHER gods BESIDES ME! How could anyone or any people possibly worship gods besides the One True God, the only God? And yet, He knew they would! And He knew, we would! He knew we would worship the provision over the Provider. He knew we would worship the seen over the Everlasting. He knew we would worship the temporal over the Eternal.

To worship God means to be wholly and reverently devoted to Him, and to express that reverence and devotion to Him in all things. A god is any person, possession or purpose that we have allowed to become the object of our attention or devotion. It may be that job or that hobby or that relationship that we have allowed to become all-consuming. If we have allowed any person, possession or purpose to become the object of our attention or devotion, we are worshiping another god besides the One True God.

The purpose of your journey through this wilderness may be all about your awakening to the reality that you have been worshiping other gods. God is jealous for the worship that is due Him. Today turn your attention and devotion to Him. See Him for Who He is. God gave this commandment as the first of the ten, because the starting place for all the others is here. Jesus said that the first and greatest commandment is to love the Lord your God with all of your heart, soul and mind; and that everything else depends upon this. Worship Him! The Father sent His Son to die on the cross so that we might be able to worship Him. God has chosen you to be His child for that purpose – that you might worship Him. He has allowed you to experience His presence – that you might worship Him. He has allowed you to witness His power – that you might worship Him. Do not worship any other gods besides Him! What adjustment do you need to make in your life today to worship Him? Do not delay any longer. There is none like Him!

* * *

36

NO FALSE IMAGES

Then God instructed the people as follows: "Do not make idols of any kind, whether in the shape of birds or animals or fish. You must never worship or bow down to them, for I, the LORD your God, am a jealous God who will not share your affection with any other god! I do not leave unpunished the sins of those who hate Me, but I punish the children for the sins of their parents to the third and fourth generations. But I lavish My love on those who love Me and obey My commands, even for a thousand generations."
Exodus 20:1, 4-6

* * *

Just as God's first commandment to the children of Israel dealt with Who they were to worship, the second commandment deals with how He is to be worshipped; the first with the Object of our worship, and the second with the orientation of our worship. On the mount that day, God was giving the people His Word, His revelation of Himself and Who He is. In this commandment He establishes that the presence of the Living God is never to be represented or revealed by anything man-made, but represented and revealed by His Word. Again God recognizes how easily we can be distracted in worshipping Him by the seen; particularly our image of what the seen should look like.

As you visit the Holy Land today, you are struck by the Christian shrines that have been built all over as reminders of events recorded in Scripture. Many of the sites are presumed to be correct, but there is no way to unquestionably test the veracity of many of them. But what you begin to quickly observe, however, as you visit these shrines is that they have become an object of worship. Those places that were intended to point people to the Person of Christ have become venerated themselves, and have become the object of attention instead of the One to whom they were intended to point.

Let me give an example that is a little closer to home. As you are proceeding on your journey through the wilderness, do you have a picture in your mind of where this journey will end? Is it clearly a God-revealed vision of where He is leading (just as He gave Joseph), or is it your picture of where you think He is leading? i have the propensity to try and run ahead of God. i get in my mind an image of where i think He is leading in my life. As a matter of fact, i begin to look at the circumstances unfolding in my life and i neatly organize them into a storyboard that tells the story with my picture as the ending. More than once, i have composed a wonderful storyboard testimony of where and how God was leading, only to find out that i was 100% wrong. i had pictured myself telling that "false" testimony to the glory of God; the only problem was it wasn't God's testimony; it was my image of it. And then when it didn't unfold, boy was i disappointed – even disappointed in God, that things hadn't turned out according to my image. And it affected my worship, because my focus shifted from Him to my image.

Let me give another example of an image we create. One of the most widely debated issues in the church today, is the issue of the use of traditional hymns versus contemporary praise songs in our worship services. This debate is dividing the body and splitting churches across Christendom. We have established images of worship – "contemporary-style", "traditional-style" or "blended style" – and we have begun to worship our image of "style of worship" instead of the true Object of our worship. When we do that we cease to give God the worship He is due; and the worship He has commanded of us.

Now in all of these examples, we did not start off worshipping a false God, but the images we created became an object of our worship; they became a false god – an idol. God told His people that was sin. It is not only an abuse of His commandment; it is an affront to His majesty. He then went on to warn His people as a part of this commandment that their sin – their false worship - will result in the punishment of their children to the third and fourth generations. But their faithfulness to this commandment in the area of their worship would result in Him lavishing His love upon future generations – "even for a thousand generations" – and that's a long time!

Why then is God taking this commandment so seriously? Because He knows that our obedience to His remaining commandments will flow out of our right relationship with Him, and that a right relationship begins at the point of our worship. Or put more succinctly, our obedience will flow out of our worship.

As we continue our journey in the wilderness, let us therefore join with the psalmist in saying *"May the words of my mouth and the thoughts of my heart be pleasing to you, O LORD, my rock and my redeemer"* (Ps 19:14 NLT). And keep me from creating any image of worship, shaped in any form. Keep my focus on You, O LORD, for You alone are worthy of my worship.

* * *

37

NO PROFANITY

*Then God instructed the people as follows: "Do not misuse the name of the LORD
your God. The LORD will not let you go unpunished if you misuse His name."*
Exodus 20:1, 7

* * *

Growing up in a Christian home, i was taught that this
commandment meant that the use of profanity, "swearing", taking
the Lord's Name in vain was a sin – and it is! Regrettably, on more than
one occasion the bar of bath soap made its way into my mouth for an
extended period, as my parents were teaching me this important
commandment. But as i have traveled further in the wilderness, i have
come to realize that there are many ways that we can misuse, or profane,
the Name of the LORD our God.

We profane the Name of the LORD when we profess a relationship with
Him with our mouth and not our heart – when we profess to be His
follower but do not turn from our iniquity. It has been said that one of the
greatest mission fields is in the church pews on Sunday morning, where
many are gathered that are profaning the name of the Lord by professing
one thing on Sunday morning and living another throughout the rest of
the week. Jesus said, *"Not all people who sound religious are really godly. They
may refer to Me as 'Lord,' but they still won't enter the Kingdom of Heaven. The
decisive issue is whether they obey my Father in heaven. On judgment day many
will tell me, 'Lord, Lord, we prophesied in Your name and cast out demons in*

Your name and performed many miracles in Your name.' But I will reply, 'I never knew you. Go away; the things you did were unauthorized'" (Matt 7:21-23).

We profane the Name of the LORD when we enter into a promise with God or to God, and then break that promise. In Ecclesiastes we read, *"So when you make a promise to God, don't delay in following through, for God takes no pleasure in fools. Keep all the promises you make to Him. It is better to say nothing than to promise something that you don't follow through on. In such cases, your mouth is making you sin. And don't defend yourself by telling the Temple messenger that the promise you made was a mistake. That would make God angry, and He might wipe out everything you have achieved"* (Eccl 5:4-6).

We profane the Name of the Lord when we enter into a pledge rashly or falsely and invoke the Name of the Lord. James wrote, *"Never take an oath, by heaven or earth or anything else. Just say a simple yes or no, so that you will not sin and be condemned for it"* (James 5:12).

We profane the Name of the Lord when we ascribe words to Him that He has not spoken. In Proverbs we read, *"Every word of God proves true. He defends all who come to Him for protection. Do not add to His words, or He may rebuke you, and you will be found a liar"* (Prov 30:5-6).

As we have already seen, our Lord has set our feet on this journey for the fulfillment of His purpose – that His Name might be glorified among all of the peoples, all of the tribes, all of the nations. All that our Lord does will lead to the glory of His Name. And our Lord jealously guards the glory of His Name. When we profane His Name, He can therefore by no means allow us to go unpunished. As you journey, if you are profaning His Name by professing a relationship with Him that you do not have, turn to Him today turning from your iniquity and you will be saved. If you are profaning His Name having broken a promise that you made in His Name, or made one rashly or falsely, seek His forgiveness and His cleansing and the forgiveness of those to whom the promise was made and where possible, make good on that promise. If you have profaned His Name by ascribing words to Him that He has not spoken, go and make the record straight, confessing your sin and seeking forgiveness.

Allow Him to transform your profanity into exaltation that honors and glorifies the Name of the LORD your God.

* * *

38

A DAY SET APART

Then God instructed the people as follows: "Remember to observe the Sabbath day
by keeping it holy. Six days a week are set apart for your daily duties and regular
work, but the seventh day is a day of rest dedicated to the LORD your God. On
that day no one in your household may do any kind of work. This includes you,
your sons and daughters, your male and female servants, your livestock, and any
foreigners living among you. For in six days the LORD made the heavens, the
earth, the sea, and everything in them; then he rested on the seventh day. That is
why the LORD blessed the Sabbath day and set it apart as holy."
Exodus 20:1, 8-11

* * *

God begins this commandment by saying, "Remember". This was not
a new commandment. God had instituted the Sabbath day at
creation when He set the seventh day apart and declared it to be a holy
day. It was a day which He had set apart to be a day of rest for Himself
from His work of creation. He completed His work in six days and rested
on the seventh. Now, our Creator, who created us in His image and knows
our frame, declares that six days are to be set apart for our daily duties
and regular work, but the seventh day must be set apart as a day of rest.
And that day must be dedicated to the LORD. As followers of Christ, the
day that we have set aside is the first day of the week – the Lord's Day – to
be not only the day of Sabbath rest but also a day of remembrance of our
Lord's resurrection. By observing this Sabbath, we imitate our God.

Over the years, a misinterpretation has emerged that says that God set apart the Sabbath to be the day of worship. We are very good at compartmentalizing our lives, but God never intended for us to compartmentalize worship. The fact of the matter is, as we have seen in the first three commandments, we are to worship our LORD every moment of every day. Our life, our work, every aspect of our existence is to be an expression of worship. Keeping the Sabbath is in fact to be an expression of our worship; but it is not intended to limit our worship. Everything God has given us, He has given us for the purpose of bringing glory to His Name – and that includes the Sabbath. i do not include this statement to suggest license that we not gather for a time of corporate worship on the Sabbath. The writer of Hebrews very clearly admonished us not to forsake the assembling of ourselves together. But do not use it in the context to limit your worship to one day. Jesus taught, *"The Sabbath was made for man, and not man for the Sabbath"* (Mark 2:27 NKJ). Therefore the Sabbath is a part of God's provision for our lives. By observing this Sabbath, we honor our God.

God gave the Israelites a very practical example of this commandment every week. For several weeks now He had been providing them with heavenly bread delivered fresh to their wilderness six days per week. On the sixth day, as you recall, He was providing them with a double portion so that there would be no need to gather provision on that seventh day. And though the manna on every other day would spoil if they tried to keep it into the next, the sixth day's manna was able to be carried forward to the seventh, because that was God's intention. In that way, He made provision for the day He had provided to be set apart for rest. That is one of the ways that God blessed the Sabbath day – He made provision for what He had already provided and now the people had to trust Him. As in all things, they (and we) experience God's blessings, as we trust Him. They would only experience God's blessing of the day of Sabbath rest, if they trusted Him for His provision for it throughout the preceding six days. By observing this Sabbath, we demonstrate our trust in our God.

The keeping of the Sabbath was in fact intended to be a sign that these truly were God's people. This was to be something unique about them that set them apart from all other peoples. Through the prophet Isaiah, God made this promise: *"Keep the Sabbath day holy. Don't pursue your own interests on that day, but enjoy the Sabbath and speak of it with delight as the LORD's holy day."* (Isa 58:13) By observing this Sabbath, we testify of our God.

The first three commandments have dealt with the love that we must have for God. This commandment deals with an expression of that love from our God and to our God through our obedience in setting apart the Sabbath day of rest. By observing this Sabbath, we express our love for our God as we obey Him.

During the period between the Old Testament and the New Testament, the Jewish religious leaders added many restrictions to the observance of the Sabbath that were not a part of God's plan (remember, we are not to add to God's words – Prov 30:6). Jesus rebuked them for their pharisaical attitude that was causing the people to miss the whole purpose for which God had intended the day. The people were so focused on the list of "do's and don'ts" that they were missing God's intended purpose for setting aside the day. The human law made the Sabbath a burden instead of the blessing God intended; an external observance instead of a delight.

Do not forget as you journey through the wilderness that God has called us to set aside this Sabbath day of rest. Do not allow the day that God has given you to become just another day of the week. As you set this day apart, you will imitate your Lord, honor your Lord, demonstrate your trust in your Lord, testify that He is your Lord, and express your love for your Lord. In so doing, you will have set it apart for His purpose – a day that is holy, acceptable unto Him.

* * *

39

LOVE YOUR NEIGHBOR

Then God instructed the people as follows: "Honor your father and mother. Then
you will live a long, full life in the land the LORD your God will give you. Do
not murder. Do not commit adultery. Do not steal. Do not testify falsely against
your neighbor. Do not covet your neighbor's house. Do not covet your neighbor's
wife, male or female servant, ox or donkey, or anything else your neighbor owns."
Exodus 20:1, 12-17

* * *

God had put first things first, and now He was putting second things
second. He was revealing His commandments in the order of His
creation. Man had a Creator before he had a neighbor. Man must learn to
love his Creator before he can possibly love his neighbor. We must learn to
love our Heavenly Father before we can possibly know how to love our
earthly father (and mother). Therefore, God had spelled out His first four
commandments on how the people must love Him. Once the people knew
what it meant to love Him, God was free to reveal to them His remaining
six commandments that dealt with how to love one another. Obedience to
these six commandments would flow, not out of their love for others but
out of their love for God and obedience to His first four commandments.
Do you see the hinge that connects all of this together? It is love for God; a
love that involves our whole heart, soul, body and mind.

The Pharisees and scribes thought they had Jesus over a barrel when they
posed this question to Him. "Teacher, which is the great commandment in

the Law?" *Jesus replied, " 'You must love the Lord your God with all your heart, all your soul, and all your mind.' This is the first and greatest commandment. A second is equally important: 'Love your neighbor as yourself.' All the other commandments and all the demands of the prophets are based on these two commandments"* (Matt 22:37-40). The second commandment that Jesus told them actually was not in the Law, it summarized the Law; and what's more, it went beyond the letter of the Law and went straight to the Father's heart of the Law.

That day on Mount Sinai God knew the propensity of this people. He knew the seed from which they had come. He had witnessed Cain dishonor his father and mother and murder his brother. God had seen Noah's son Ham dishonor his father by looking on his nakedness. God had heard Abraham lie to Pharaoh that Sarai was not his wife. God had seen Jacob's, and his mother Rebekah's, deception of Isaac to rob Esau of his father's blessing. He had witnessed the sons of Jacob dishonor their father and sell their brother into slavery. He had seen Jacob's son Judah commit adultery with his daughter-in-law Tamar. He knew that because of their sin nature they were disposed and inclined to sin against Him and to sin against one another.

So God spelled out some basics on what it meant to love one another. First we must honor our parents. He did not make that commandment conditional on their worthiness based upon their performance, but in honor of their position as parents. We will never truly be able to love others as we should until first we love God and second we love and honor our parents. Now God has blessed me with godly parents who love the Lord and have always demonstrated their love for me; and i truly do count them as a blessing from the Lord. And i know that this is not the case for many of you. But God says, "Honor them." Love them unconditionally. Some of you are saying, "I can't." That's true, but God can and does, and He will love them through you if you will let Him. We can't love others until we first love Him and part of loving Him is allowing Him to love others through us. And it starts with your parents. i didn't say that. God said it.

Next, He said no murder. That not only includes a bullet in the heart (murder), but also a knife in the back (character assassination), and all the many ways we can murder with our deeds and our mouths. He said no adultery. That includes not only sex outside of marriage; it includes cheating and immorality of every kind. He said no stealing or lying. And He said no coveting – that means no jealousy, no envy, no lust – no purposing in our hearts, even if we don't follow through with action. Jesus taught that it is not only our actions but also our very thoughts that defile us (Mark 7:21-23).

None of us made it through that list unscathed. All of us have sinned against our neighbor because all of us are sinners. God gave the people His Law, His Standard, to reveal to them, and to us, that no one can live up to God's standard. We have all fallen short. No one can live that sinless life. That's why we need a Savior. That's why the Father sent His Son, Jesus.

And if i have repented of my sin and turned to follow Christ, then i can say with the apostle Paul, "I myself no longer live, but Christ lives in me. So I live my life in this earthly body by trusting in the Son of God, who loved me and gave himself for me" (Gal 2:20). Then because of Jesus living in me and through me, no matter where i am in my journey through the wilderness, i can love my neighbor.

* * *

40

A HEALTHY FEAR

When the people heard the thunder and the loud blast of the horn, and when they saw the lightning and the smoke billowing from the mountain, they stood at a distance, trembling with fear. And they said to Moses, "You tell us what God says, and we will listen. But don't let God speak directly to us. If he does, we will die!" "Don't be afraid," Moses said, "for God has come in this way to show you his awesome power. From now on, let your fear of him keep you from sinning.
Exodus 20:18-20

* * *

The thunder, the lightening, the smoke, and the long loud blast of the horn all served as a reminder to the people of His awesome power. They were standing in the presence of Yahweh – the Lord God Jehovah. And though they stood at a distance, they trembled with fear. This is the first time recorded in Scripture that the Israelites trembled with fear before God. They had trembled with fear when the Egyptian army was preparing to attack them at the Red Sea. But their fear was in response to the intimidating force of their enemy behind them. They had trembled with fear as they walked through the walls of water on the dry seabed of the Red Sea. But their fear was in response to the overwhelming mountains of water beside them. They were now in the third month since they had left Egypt. Every day for almost three months, God had demonstrated His presence through the pillar of cloud, the pillar of fire, His miracles of protection and His miracles of provision. But the response of His people to His presence to this point would best have been described as complacency, mixed with extended periods of grumbling and complaining, together with the occasional shout of praise and joy in response to His miracles. But on this day their eyes were opened and they saw God for Who He was and their fear was in response to His overwhelming majesty before them.

We too have lost the vision of the awesome power of the Lord God Jehovah. Yes, He is our loving Heavenly Father. He is Jehovah Shalom, our God of Peace. He is Jehovah Jireh, our Lord God Provider. But He is also El Shaddai, the Lord God Almighty. For how many days have we passively walked with Him, indifferent and complacent in the midst of His presence? Oh, we will praise Him for the miracles and we will thank Him for the miraculous provision, but we do not fear Him.

There are two types of fear – one is healthy and one is harmful. Harmful fear is a panic-stricken dread or terror. If we are a child of God, we are to cast all of our harmful fears upon Him. As His child, there is no enemy that can defeat or destroy us apart from His will. There is nothing that can overcome us unless He, in His sovereignty, permits it. And if He permits it, He will give us the strength and the stamina and the grace to endure it. Therefore, He tells us to fear not, but to trust Him; casting all fears upon Him. However, if i am not a child of God, i will stand before God with terror and with dread, because i stand before Him as a condemned man. That fear will cause me to either turn to Him in repentance, or unfortunately in too many cases, to try to hide from Him in denial and rebellion.

Healthy fear is a reverence and respect. As a child of God, we are to live our lives with a fear of God. Jethro had counseled Moses to seek men who fear God, to serve the people A fear of God will cause me to live my life in the constant awareness that my every thought, attitude and action is under His scrutiny. God allowed the people that day to witness His awesome power, not that they might be afraid and run from Him in terror, but so they might ever be mindful to live their lives before Him in reverence and respect.

It is interesting to me to note that God had not allowed the eyes of the people to be opened to see Him in this way until they had journeyed for almost three months. God knew what they needed to see and experience before they would be ready to see Him for Who He is. They needed to taste the bitter waters made sweet. They needed to taste the bread of heaven. They needed to experience His victory over the Egyptians and the Amalekites. They needed to have come to the place that they knew that they were wholly dependent upon Him. **You see, too often, the God we want is the God we think we need.** And when we're living our lives in the comfort zone where everything is going smooth, even if it's in the bondage of Egypt, we settle into a complacency and an indifference to Who God is and Who He desires to be in our lives. Then after He has led us out on our journey into the wilderness, we begin to understand our dependence upon Him. As we then begin to better understand how much we need Him, we begin to better understand Who He is. And as we begin to better understand and see Him for Who He is, then we will begin to learn what it means to live in the fear of the Lord God Jehovah – our El Shaddai!

* * *

41

LEAVE THE CROWD, CLIMB THE MOUNTAIN

As the people stood in the distance, Moses entered into the deep darkness where God was.
Exodus 20:21

* * *

M oses had no idea all that God was about to tell Him. As we see recorded in the remainder of chapter 20 as well as chapters 21 through 23, God began to set forth to Moses a detailed account of His ordinances for the people under the framework of His ten command-ments. He gave specific instruction on how the people were to present sacrifices to Him, how they were to honor Him and remember His acts through the ceremonial feasts, and how they were to treat one another. Moses heard it; the people would only hear about it.

As we look at the picture that day on the mountain, i am struck by the contrast – the people stood in the distance, but Moses climbed higher, entering deeper into God's presence. The people stood apart as a crowd in the distance; but Moses entered in as an intimate in His presence. The people were satisfied to have experienced the thunder and the lighten-ing; but Moses desired to hear His voice and see His face. The people were content to stand in the fear of God; but Moses sought the comfort that came by drawing closer to God. The people walked away with greater knowledge that day; but Moses entered into a deeper under-standing that day. The people got a glimpse of the big picture at a distance; but Moses entered into the deeper things that can only be learned in God's presence.

i am reminded of a day almost 1,500 years later. There was another crowd. They also were children of Israel. They had witnessed God's power through a dramatic display - the *"healing of all kinds of sickness and all kinds of disease"* (Matt 4:23). The people didn't know quite what to make of this Jesus, but they gathered by the multitudes that day at a mountain overlooking the Sea of Galilee. And seeing the multitudes, Jesus went up higher, and His disciples came up to where He was. The disciples knew that day that they couldn't stay where they were and experience the presence of Jesus. Oh, they might be able to see Him; they might even be able to hear Him from a distance, but they didn't want to know Jesus from a distance. They wanted to know Jesus close up. They didn't want to risk missing anything that Jesus had to say. They didn't want to have to strain to hear Him. They wanted to hear Him clearly, even if He whispered. They didn't only want to hear the parables that He told the crowds. They wanted to hear the explanations that He gave to those who were close to Him. So they left the crowd and climbed the mountain. They made whatever adjustment was necessary to be right where Jesus was. And that is what Moses did that day at Sinai; he left the crowd and climbed the mountain, entering deeper into God's presence.

As Moses entered deeper into where God was, it became darker. It wasn't darker for Moses; he was entering closer into the presence of God. And i believe that God shone brighter than the noonday sun on his path and all that was around him. The ones it became darker for were the people in the crowd. As they stayed where they were and Moses moved further away from them into the presence of God, it became more difficult for them to see Moses – to see where he was, or what he was doing, or what he was experiencing. And later, when he returned to them, no matter how much he might have tried to explain what He saw, what He heard and what He experienced, the people couldn't understand. They hadn't been there. They hadn't experienced it. They couldn't even see it. Moses was too far removed from them. From where the people were, he was in the dark.

Our Lord is inviting each and every one of us to come up the mountain and enter deeper into His presence. James wrote, *"Draw close to God, and God will draw close to you..."* (James 4:8). In order to experience greater intimacy in your relationship with God, you must be prepared to climb higher and enter deeper. There are things that He can only teach you as you climb higher. There is an understanding of Him that you will only have once you climb higher. There are things He will only let you see after you climb higher. God set your feet on this journey through the wilderness so that you might experience Him in ways that you never have before. But in order to do that, there will be times that He will lead you away from your fellow sojourners. What is that adjustment that He is calling you to make to enter deeper into His presence? The crowd probably won't make the adjustment. They may be satisfied to stand right where they are at a distance. Trust Him! It's worth it. He's worth it! Leave the crowd, climb the mountain!

* * *

42

ALL THE WAY THERE

"See, I am sending my angel before you to lead you safely to the land I have
prepared for you. Pay attention to him, and obey all of his instructions. Do not
rebel against him, for he will not forgive your sins. He is my representative--he
bears my name. But if you are careful to obey him, following all my instructions,
then I will be an enemy to your enemies, and I will oppose those who oppose you.
For my angel will go before you and bring you into the land.... You must serve
only the LORD your God. If you do, I will bless you with food and water, and I
will keep you healthy."
Exodus 23:20-23, 25

* * *

"Watch and see. I am sending My angel before you to lead you." If you are journeying through the wilderness, i can't think of a more reassuring word you could receive from God. As i write this, my family and i are in the midst of just such a journey that we know God has led us to begin. It has been over two months since we left the ministry where God had allowed us to serve Him for almost twelve years. We anticipated serving our Lord in that place until He raptured or retired us. But He began to show us very clearly that He was calling us to leave our comfort zone and go. Our next question didn't seem to be that unreasonable. We asked, "Lord, where would you like us to go? To the ends of the earth? Wherever it is we will go. Lord, just show us." But i will confess that we weren't prepared for His answer. His answer rocked the very foundation of our souls. "I am not calling you to go to a place; I am calling you to come to Me – to follow Me. Leave from where you are and follow Me to a

place I will show you." Now i will confess to you that it is one thing to
read about God saying that to Abraham, or even the children of Israel; it is
quite another to hear Him say that to you. i will never forget the night we
as a family gathered to discuss the next step God was leading us to take.
As one by one we affirmed to one another a clear understanding that God
was calling us to take just such a step – a step from the known to the
unseen; a step from the shore into the boat; and a step out of the boat onto
the water. And we knew that to delay in our obedience would be disobedience to God.

The Israelites also were in the third month of their journey through the
wilderness. God promised them that He was sending His angel to lead
them. He promised that he had already prepared the land to which He
was leading them. He promised that if they were attentive and obedient to
all of His instructions they would safely arrive at the land. He promised to
provide them with food and water and to keep them in good health.

The Representative that God sent to lead them was no created being. The
Representative that God sent bore the name of God. God will share His
Name and His glory with no other. God was sending His Spirit to lead
them. His Spirit, who leads us in all truth and leads us to all truth. His
Spirit, who can only tell us what He has heard the Father say (John 16:13).
His Spirit, who empowers us to accomplish all that He leads us in. His
Spirit, who convicts us of sin, but does not forgive us of sin (only the
Father can forgive us through the sacrifice of the Son). God promised that
His Spirit would go before them, opposing those who opposed them and
bringing them into the land.

The same God who led you to begin this journey is the same God who
will lead you through this journey. The same promise that He gave His
children that day in the wilderness is the same promise that He gives to
us. Why did He again remind them at this point in their journey? Because
He knew that they needed to be reminded. He knew that they needed to
be reassured. He knew that they, like us, could become weary in the
journey and distracted by the discomfort and difficulties of the wilderness. He knew that they, like us, would look at the provision that
remained and question how they could possibly continue any further. He
knew that they, like us, could begin to question why they had begun this
journey. Had it truly been God that had called them to leave their homes
and to venture out into the wilderness? God knew that they, like us, could
begin to lose sight of the promises He had given them when they stepped

out. So God gave them a mid-journey reminder. He renewed His commitment to them. He assured them that if they would continue to walk by faith, following Him, they would inhabit the land. He sealed His commitment to them by sending His Spirit.

God has sealed His commitment to you by sending you His Holy Spirit. His Spirit will go before you to guide you; He will go behind you to protect you; and He will indwell you to empower and encourage you. Yes, take heart in the journey, God has sent His Spirit to lead us into the land that He has prepared for us. And He will lead us – all the way there!

* * *

43

NO COMPROMISES

"I will… drive out the Hivites, Canaanites, and Hittites. But I will not do this all in one year because the land would become a wilderness, and the wild animals would become too many to control. I will drive them out a little at a time until your population has increased enough to fill the land. And I will fix your boundaries from the Red Sea to the Mediterranean Sea, and from the southern deserts to the Euphrates River. I will help you defeat the people now living in the land, and you will drive them out ahead of you. Make no treaties with them and have nothing to do with their gods. Do not even let them live among you! If you do, they will infect you with their sin of idol worship, and that would be disastrous for you."
Exodus 23:28-33

* * *

God was giving His people clear instructions on what would occur when they entered into His Promised Land. Though almost all of these people would miss seeing the fulfillment of this promise due to their subsequent disobedience, this instruction was as sure now as it would be on the day they entered the land forty years hence. And remember, at the time God gave them this promise, its fulfillment would have only been weeks away if they had obeyed. God was going before His people to drive out the enemies. But God even had a purpose for the enemies. Unknown to the Hivites, Canaanites and Hittites, God was using them to tend the land – to keep the land from becoming overgrown by the wilderness and overrun by the wild animals. From a distance it could have appeared that the enemies were in control of the land, but God was always in control of the land. He had only allowed them to be there for the furtherance of His purpose.

i don't know what enemy you see up ahead in the land that God has promised to you, or even on the path of your wilderness journey. But take heart, they don't control the land, God does! He has only allowed them to be there for His purpose. When His time comes for them to be gone, they will be gone! But in the meantime God is accomplishing His purpose through them.

In that light, God was very clearly showing the Israelites that He would enable them to defeat the enemies. Now notice, He said, "I will help you." Now that meant they would have to work for victory, but they were assured of success if they obeyed God. God had not promised to give them the land on a silver platter. They would have to work. It wouldn't be instant success; it would be one victory at a time. We live in a day, time and culture where we expect everything immediately – fast food, immediate satisfaction, and instant success. Then we become discouraged when God does not work in our lives in that fashion. But God did not promise the Israelites instant success, and very rarely, if ever, does He promise us instant success. But He will accomplish it in His timing and He will require us to work for it. And His timing will be perfect.

God knew that the people would be tempted to compromise with the enemy. They would be tempted to take the shortcut to accomplish the victory and inhabit the land. They would be tempted to avoid the work of the battle and the risk of the battle. What risk? God had assured them of victory! But how often do we compromise to avoid the work and the risk of the battle when God has clearly assured us of victory? God has given us everything that is required to accomplish the work – the resources, the strength and the talent. He has equipped us and will empower us just as He promised to do for the Israelites. Our victory is assured just as was theirs. There is no risk; there is only a promise of victory! There is to be no compromise.

You see those shortcuts that God knew they would be tempted to take would result in consequences that would not only impact their lives, but the lives of generations to come. God knows that the shortcuts we are tempted to take will result in consequences in our lives and the generations that follow us. God also knows that the compromises we are tempted to make are subtle; they are "small" steps. They are steps that slowly lead down a slippery slope – steps that will go down to death; steps that will lay hold of Sheol (Prov 5:5). God's boundary is clear. He told them – no treaties, no cohabitation, no compromise. If you do you will be infected by their sin. That's what sin does, it infects, it inhabits and it destroys!

God has told us, *"There is a way that seems right to a man, but its end is the way of death"* (Prov 14:12). If you are a follower of Jesus, God has called you unto Himself. He has set you apart as one of His children. God's plan is not for you to assimilate and blend in with the people around you. God has called us to be salt and light. He has told us to not compromise in His work, His ways, or His Word. We are His ambassadors. We have not been authorized to negotiate compromises! We live in a time where we are seeing the degeneration of churches around the country as they compromise God's work, His ways and His Word. God has called us to stand against the enemy; that He will defeat them. As you journey through the wilderness or as you enter into the land of promise, make no compromises to what God has told you. His victory is assured. Follow Him!

* * *

44
___

WHEN GOD SPEAKS, WRITE IT DOWN

*When Moses had announced to the people all the teachings and regulations the
LORD had given him, they answered in unison, "We will do everything the
LORD has told us to do." Then Moses carefully wrote down all the LORD's
instructions.
And the LORD said to Moses, "Come up to me on the mountain. Stay there while
I give you the tablets of stone that I have inscribed with my instructions and
commands. Then you will teach the people from them."*
Exodus 24:3-4, 12-13

* * *

It wasn't enough to just hear God's instruction, or even to announce
God's instruction, we must write down God's instruction and then we
must respond to God's instruction. In this article we will look at the para-
mountcy of writing down God's instruction.

Years ago, God brought a brother in Christ, Bryan, into my life to disciple
this middle-aged spiritual babe. And though i had been attending church
since nine months prior to my birth, when Bryan challenged me to have a
quiet time, i was certain that he was referring to a power nap on a Sunday
afternoon. i hadn't put the whole thing together in terms of spending a
time alone with God. Of course, i had heard about reading the Bible and
prayer; but to me those were disjointed activities. Though i knew that the
Bible was God's Word, i still viewed it as just a Book – albeit the most
important Book that had ever been written. What i was missing was that

God's Word is His revelation of Himself to us. That His Word is not merely His teachings and His regulations, it is His revelation of Who He is and His character. Through His Word He enables us to do more than know <u>about</u> Him, He enables us to <u>know</u> Him. As we spend time in His Word, we're not spending time with a Book, we're spending time with a Person. It is not time with "It"; it is time with "Him". He desires for us as His children to know Him, to know Him more, and to know Him more intimately. This brother challenged me that God was going to speak to me through His word; and He went on to say (quoting Henry Blackaby), "If the God of the universe is going to speak to you, it is worth writing down."

He then challenged me to set aside a time each day for the next twenty-one days. He told me to enter into that time with an open Bible, and a journal of some type to record what God said to me through His Word. Since i had never done anything like this before, i didn't know how to begin, Bryan encouraged me to start in the Gospel of John (just a chapter each day – the Gospel of John has twenty-one chapters), to come without an agenda of what i wanted to hear from God and to ask God to prepare my heart to meet with Him. i'll never forget that first day. i made preparations the night before. i got out my Bible, my notebook and my pen. i entered into this with a mild sense of apprehension. i thought Bryan was maybe a little on the edge about all of this – but i'd committed to do this for twenty-one days. i read that first chapter, wrote down a one sentence summary of what i had read, and determined that i could do that for twenty more days.

i continued that pattern each day until day ten. On that day, i heard the Lord say to me, "*My sheep know My voice.*" i heard Him speak to me more clearly than any conversation i had ever had. i had accepted Jesus as my Savior when i was six years old, but that day at the age of thirty-six, i heard His voice. From that day forward i stopped having a quiet time for Bryan and started to have a quiet time because i wanted to spend time with God and hear His voice and know Him more intimately.

Over the years, the Lord has continued to show me the importance of writing down what He says during our times together. First, it becomes a permanent record to help me remember. i, like you, am prone to forget whatever i do not write down. What God has shown me i am accountable for; therefore i must be faithful to write it down to help me remember. i can't begin to tell you the number of times i have had to go back and reread my journal in the midst of a journey to be reminded of the promises that God has given me. Second, it helps me to better understand what God has shown me – to reinforce His truth. Writing down that truth helps me to process, clarify and personalize His truth in my life. Third, as i look back over a prolonged period, i can begin to see a pattern of what God is revealing to me about Himself and how His revelation aligns with the circumstances i am encountering as i continue in the path on which He has set my feet.

God had Moses write down His instructions for the people. God, Himself, wrote down with His own finger His commandments and instructions for the people on the stone tablets. The words were written down as a permanent reminder, reinforcement and revelation of God's Person, His Promise and His Purpose. Write it down, lest you forget. Write it down, lest you misunderstand. Write it down, lest you fail to pass it on. As you journey through your wilderness – God is speaking! Write it Down!

* * *

45

WHEN GOD SPEAKS, RESPOND

*When Moses had announced to the people all the teachings and regulations the
LORD had given him, they answered in unison, "We will do everything the
LORD has told us to do." Then Moses carefully wrote down all the LORD's
instructions.
And the LORD said to Moses, "Come up to me on the mountain. Stay there while
I give you the tablets of stone that I have inscribed with my instructions and
commands. Then you will teach the people from them."*
Exodus 24:3-4, 12-13

* * *

As we've already seen, it isn't enough to just hear God's instruction,
or even to announce God's instruction, we must write down God's
instruction and then we must respond to His instruction.

When Moses announced God's teachings and regulations to the people,
the people were faced with a decision. How would they respond? Not,
would they respond? We cannot encounter God and not respond. Even
the absence of a response is a response. There is no such thing as being
neutral. We either receive and accept God's truth, His revelation of
Himself, or we do not. We cannot be ambivalent. Ambivalence is rejection
of Who God is and what He has said.

The people responded in unison, "We will do everything the LORD has told us to do." These were the right words, but the wrong response. Because God knew their hearts; He knew their intent.

As the parents of two teenagers, my wife and i have learned that there are four possible responses to any instruction or regulation we set forth in our household:

- Yes, and I truly mean it
- Yes, and I don't mean it
- No
- Silence, which is really a "no" answer

Let's look at these in the reverse order that i have listed them in. Silence, and/or "no" are a straightforward pronouncement of my intentions to disobey. i am either literally or figuratively shaking my proverbial fist and saying "i don't care what you say, i'm not doing it." One of the greatest examples of this in Scripture is Jonah. There was no question in Jonah's mind of what God was directing him to do, and Jonah said, "I am not going to Nineveh." Though i can't support the disobedience of this approach, i can appreciate the honesty. But God is not looking for honesty; He's looking for obedience.

The next answer "Yes, and I don't mean it" is saying one of two things. Either, i don't want to obey you so i'll say "yes" to get you off my back now and deal with the consequences for my lack of obedience later. This is deceptive disobedience. i know from the outset that i have no plan to obey. The other meaning of this answer is, i want to obey you and i will obey you to the extent i am able to obey you. Now, if other things get in my way and prevent me from finishing the task, it's really not my fault – i wanted to obey and i tried to obey so i get an "A" for effort – right? Wrong! This is faithless disobedience. i lacked the conviction to make whatever adjustment was necessary to obey. This is how the children of Israel were responding. God had established a standard for their obedience that was perfection. There was no way they could accomplish it on their own. But instead of responding by asking God to give them the ability to walk in obedience, they responded by saying "We'll obey --- to the best of our ability." They left an "out" clause for themselves that they could take whenever the going got tough. And it wasn't very long before they exercised their "out" clause. But remember, disobedience no matter how we try to justify it is still disobedience.

The only correct response to God is "Yes, LORD, whatever You would have me do, i will do." That means whatever adjustment He would have us make, we make. God has uniquely equipped us in a way that the Israelites were not equipped. In their case, the Holy Spirit was going before them to guide their steps. In our case, if we are followers of Jesus, His Holy Spirit indwells within us, not only guiding our steps but also enabling us to walk obediently and victoriously.

If God has spoken, He has clearly revealed His best for us. He will never lead us in anything less than our best. If God has spoken, He has already enabled and empowered us to walk in His best. He will never lead us in anything that He will not enable us to complete. If God has spoken, we must then respond in obedience with an unequivocal "yes", trusting Him for the provision and completion of all that He has begun. What has God said to you on your journey in the wilderness? You must respond!

* * *

46

AN APPOINTMENT WITH GOD

And the LORD said to Moses, "Come up to me on the mountain. Stay there while I give you the tablets of stone that I have inscribed with my instructions and commands...." Then Moses went up the mountain, and the cloud covered it. And the glorious presence of the LORD rested upon Mount Sinai, and the cloud covered it for six days. On the seventh day the LORD called to Moses from the cloud.... Then Moses disappeared into the cloud as he climbed higher up the mountain. He stayed on the mountain forty days and forty nights.... Then as the LORD finished speaking with Moses on Mount Sinai, he gave him the two stone tablets inscribed with the terms of the covenant, written by the finger of God.
Exodus 24:12, 15-16, 18; 31:18

* * *

God set the appointment. He established the time, the place and the duration. He selected the attendee and He extended the invitation. God set the agenda and He led the meeting. The appointment did not commence until God began to speak, and it wasn't concluded until God was finished.

Moses waited in that mid-mountain waiting room for six days before he was invited to climb higher for that forty-day meeting. Think of that wait time the next time you are sitting in your doctor's reception area! i find myself asking the question, "Would i wait that patiently for six days?" The fact-of-the-matter is God does allow us to wait in His waiting room. The reasons for the wait are often unclear. But i must hold onto the simple truth that He is God, and i am not. It has been said that, with God, timing is more important than time. And His timing is perfect. God knew that for whatever reason Moses was not going to be prepared to hear all that God was going to say to him prior to the moment God ushered him up that mountain on the seventh day. It wasn't that God wasn't ready sooner; it was that He knew Moses was not. And as i sit in the waiting room, that is the case in my life. The waiting room is that place where God is preparing me for my encounter (my appointment) with Him. He is using that place and that time to peel away any hindrances that might prevent me from fully encountering Him. He is revealing any unconfessed sin, removing any distractions, redirecting my focus and refining my ability to hear Him. What God will reveal to us in just such an encounter is too important for us to enter into unprepared. And He knows the exact preparation that is required. Therefore i must wait patiently, diligently, attentively and responsively to Him and all that He is doing. Then in His perfect timing, He will invite me to climb higher and join Him.

Can you imagine forty days in the presence of God? Now i know that you may be thinking that you have attended worship services that seemed like they lasted for forty days, but that's not what i'm talking about. i don't believe Moses was even once tempted to look at his "calendar wrist watch" to see what day or time it was. You see when we truly enter into the presence of the Eternal God, i believe time will stand still. We will be so gripped by His presence and awed by His power that we will be blinded to all else. As Moses listened, God unfolded the details of the tabernacle that the children of Israel were to construct. This would be His dwelling place among His people. No detail would be left to chance or subject to interpretation. God would leave no room for doubt or debate.

How often do we attempt to set the agenda for an appointment with God? We set the time, the place, the duration and the agenda; and we don't understand why God doesn't show up. What's worse, sometimes we don't even realize that He hasn't shown up. And when He does, we're so preoccupied with our agenda, we miss hearing what He has to say to us and we miss the sheer enjoyment of being in His presence. Or how many times do we miss God's invitation to have an appointment with Him due to our busyness or self-centeredness. So we never show up or allow Him to prepare us for that time with Him.

Fellow sojourner, here is what i want to challenge you to do. God has brought you on this journey through the wilderness because He desires to meet with you in a way you've never met with Him before. Ask God if you can have an appointment with Him. Let Him set the time, the place, the duration and the agenda. Make whatever adjustment you need to make in your life to keep that appointment. Ask Him and allow Him to do whatever is required to prepare you for that appointment. Is this all sounding a little scary to you? Trust Him. He is your Lord God Jehovah. He desires for you to spend time with Him – but on His terms. Then keep the appointment; allow God to lead the meeting and allow Him to use that time to construct and enlarge the tabernacle of His presence in your life. He will work out the details and He won't leave any margin for error.

* * *

47

ANY OLD "GOD" WON'T DO

*Moses told the other leaders, "Stay here and wait for us until we come back. If
there are any problems while I am gone, consult with Aaron and Hur, who are
here with you." ...Then Moses disappeared into the cloud as he climbed higher up
the mountain. He stayed on the mountain forty days and forty nights. ...When
Moses failed to come back down the mountain right away, the people went to
Aaron. "Look," they said, "make us some gods who can lead us. This man Moses,
who brought us here from Egypt, has disappeared. We don't know what has
happened to him." So Aaron said, "Tell your wives and sons and daughters to
take off their gold earrings, and then bring them to me." All the people obeyed
Aaron and brought him their gold earrings. Then Aaron took the gold, melted it
down, and molded and tooled it into the shape of a calf. The people exclaimed, "O
Israel, these are the gods who brought you out of Egypt!"*
Exodus 24:14, 18; 32:1-4

* * *

A s Moses was leaving to meet with God on the mountain, he told the
people that if any questions came up or problems developed while
he and Joshua were gone, the people should consult with Aaron and Hur.
You remember Aaron and Hur – Moses' brother and brother-in-law. These
were the men that had lifted up their brother Moses' hands that day on
the hill overlooking Rephidim – the day the Amalekites were defeated.
These men were a part of Moses' inner circle. If anyone had seen the hand
of God moving on behalf of His people throughout the exodus from Egypt
and the journey through the wilderness, these men had. Aaron had been
designated by God to be Moses' spokesperson to the people. i am certain

that Aaron and Hur had both been near Moses' side at every critical venture along the way. And now comes their opportunity to shine - Moses puts them in charge until he and Joshua return.

Few of us can imagine what it was like to be thrust into a position of leadership of over one million people. Though the people had only recently pledged to trust God, this is still that same group of grumbling and complaining people that were ready to stone Moses just a few weeks back. So Aaron and Hur had their work cut out for them. And since Moses hadn't indicated how long he would be gone, i would imagine that neither of them thought it would be forty plus days. i would also imagine that when hours became days and days became weeks they started to wonder when, and perhaps if, Moses would return.

Then came the decisive test for Aaron and Hur. The people were grousing that Moses and Joshua had disappeared and probably would never return. Maybe they had gone ahead without them. Maybe they had been zapped by one of those lightening bolts. Whatever had happened, they determined they were not coming back and the God of Abraham, Isaac, Jacob and Moses was not reliable. They needed a leader that they could see, and they definitely needed a god that they could see. So they were looking for a leader who could point them to just such a god – a god they could look upon and touch and carry around with them. Any old god would do, as long as they could see it. So Aaron and Hur had a choice – either lead the people where the people wanted to go; or the people were going to find another leader. Now i'm not sure why Aaron and Hur didn't call out to God at that point. That is what they had seen Moses do every time the people acted in that way. Perhaps they thought God was busy talking to Moses so He wouldn't hear them. Or perhaps they thought they couldn't interrupt Him. Or maybe they thought only Moses could talk to God. Or maybe they feared that Moses had truly been zapped by lightening and turned into a crispy critter; how could they trust a God like that? So instead of trusting the One who had delivered them time and again, instead of calling upon Jehovah, they did the worst possible thing a leader can do, instead of looking to God and leading the people, they turned from God and followed the people – all the way to disobedience.

i think it is fitting that they shaped the gold into an image of a calf. i don't know a lot about cows, but everything i do know tells me that they do not rank very high on the animal intelligence scale. i mean, what do cows do all day? They stand around and chew their cud. Whenever we stop

worshipping the God who created us, we start creating a god to worship
in our own image. A god who stands around chewing his cud probably fit
the image of the people pretty well. And the greatest tragedy was that
they offered sacrifices to it and worshipped it. They stopped looking to the
God who is and started looking to the god they had created.

About now, your halo is fitting pretty tight on your head and you are
shaking your head piously at the stupidity and sinfulness of this people
and you are wondering why God doesn't just zap them all. (We'll talk
about why later.) But the fact-of-the-matter is, there have been times in our
life when our actions indicated that "any old god would do". We have
been tempted to place our trust in things that our hands have made; we
have been tempted to place our trust in our riches or our position or our
possessions or our abilities. We have been on the verge of shaping a god in
our image and worshiping it.

Let me call out to you before you do. Remember the Lord God Jehovah.
He alone is God. There is none like Him. Do not turn to the things of this
world. Keep your heart and your head pointed steadfastly toward Him.
Trust Him that what He has promised He will accomplish. He has not
abandoned you or forsaken you. The God who led you into this wilderness will lead you out. Any old god won't do – only the One True God!

* * *

48

WHY DIDN'T GOD STOP THEM?

When Moses failed to come back down the mountain right away, the people went to Aaron. "Look," they said, "make us some gods who can lead us. This man Moses, who brought us here from Egypt, has disappeared. We don't know what has happened to him." So Aaron said, "Tell your wives and sons and daughters to take off their gold earrings, and then bring them to me." All the people obeyed Aaron and brought him their gold earrings. Then Aaron took the gold, melted it down, and molded and tooled it into the shape of a calf. The people exclaimed, "O Israel, these are the gods who brought you out of Egypt!" When Aaron saw how excited the people were about it, he built an altar in front of the calf and announced, "Tomorrow there will be a festival to the LORD!" So the people got up early the next morning to sacrifice burnt offerings and peace offerings. After this, they celebrated with feasting and drinking, and indulged themselves in pagan revelry. Then the LORD told Moses, "Quick! Go down the mountain! The people you brought from Egypt have defiled themselves."
Exodus 32:1-7

* * *

It had been about forty days since the people had made the commitment, "We will certainly do everything the LORD asks of us." God had then clearly told them in His first commandment that they were to worship no other gods besides Him; and His second that they were not to make idols of any kind, including in the form of animals, nor were they to worship or bow down before images made by man.

Now a little over a month later, God is finishing giving His detailed instructions to Moses regarding the building of a wilderness tabernacle, the dwelling place for His presence. At some point in God's unveiling of His plan to Moses, He observes the Israelites coming to Aaron and requesting that he make an image of god for them to worship. At this point, God did not make mention of what He was seeing to Moses. He continued to observe their blatant disobedience to His commandment without making comment. Then He observed Aaron's spineless response to their request as he knowingly compromised and disobeyed God's Word. God silently watched as the people brought their offerings of gold. He saw Aaron melt the gold and mold it into the shape of a calf. He heard the people excitedly proclaim that this was the god who had brought them out of Egypt.

It is important that we realize that as God was seeing and hearing all of this, He never skipped a beat. He continued to unfold His plan to Moses. **God will permit no one and no thing to keep Him from accomplishing His appointed task – even the disobedience of His people!**

The second important insight into God's character we must see here is - **God will not prevent us from being knowingly disobedient to Him.** He is God! He could have very easily stopped them in their tracks at any point along the way, but God gave them, as He gives us, the freedom to choose to disobey. Now i believe that God does sovereignly intervene to protect us from unknowingly disobeying Him. i thank God that He protects me from my own stupidity! If the desire of my heart is to obey Him, but i am proceeding in a way that is contrary to His Word due to a lack of knowledge in my head, God will make sure that i am given that knowledge. He will seize my attention. He will surround me with Christian brothers or sisters that will point me in His ways. He will do whatever it takes to align the action of my head with the desire of my heart (assuming my heart is truly desiring to seek Him and obey Him). But God will never override our decision to be <u>knowingly</u> disobedient to Him. And remember God knows our hearts. We may be able to deceptively plead ignorance to man, but we will never be able to deceive God. Let there be no mistake; the people knew they were disobeying God's commands. Aaron knew he was disobeying God's commands.

And still God continued to watch as the people made preparations to offer burnt sacrifices and peace offerings to that golden calf. He continued as they celebrated and indulged in their pagan revelry.

Then, when God had concluded outlining His plan to Moses – in His time and not before – God prepared to respond to the disobedience of His people. Here is a third truth that we must grasp. **God alone controls His timing – neither our disobedience nor our obedience will alter His timing or force Him into action.** Don't ever confuse God's silence as being His tacit approval of our disobedience, and never assume that He is ignoring our disobedience. God will never wink at our sin. God will always deal with His people regarding our disobedience – for the sake of His Name and His glory – but He will do so in His time and His way.

God knew that these people were going to disobey long before He called Moses up the mountain. In God's perfect will, He desired that His people obey; in His permissive will, He allowed them to choose to disobey; and in His sovereignty He knew which they would choose. That's why the Father sent the Son. He knew our propensity to disobey. He knew that left to our own devices we would choose to disobey. So He sent His Son to show us how to make the right choices. He sent His Son to cleanse us of our sin from the disobedience of our wrong choices. He sent His Son to enable us to walk in that path of right choices. No, He didn't stop them. He doesn't stop us. But He made a Way. Now the choice is ours.

* * *

49

THE DAY GOD CHANGED HIS MIND

Then the LORD told Moses, "Quick! Go down the mountain! The people you brought from Egypt have defiled themselves. They have already turned from the way I commanded them to live. They have made an idol shaped like a calf, and they have worshiped and sacrificed to it. They are saying, 'These are your gods, O Israel, who brought you out of Egypt.'" Then the LORD said, "I have seen how stubborn and rebellious these people are. Now leave me alone so my anger can blaze against them and destroy them all. Then I will make you, Moses, into a great nation instead of them." But Moses pleaded with the LORD his God not to do it. "O LORD!" he exclaimed. "Why are you so angry with your own people whom you brought from the land of Egypt with such great power and mighty acts? The Egyptians will say, 'God tricked them into coming to the mountains so he could kill them and wipe them from the face of the earth.' Turn away from your fierce anger. Change your mind about this terrible disaster you are planning against your people! Remember your covenant with your servants--Abraham, Isaac, and Jacob. You swore by your own self, 'I will make your descendants as numerous as the stars of heaven. Yes, I will give them all of this land that I have promised to your descendants, and they will possess it forever.' " So the LORD withdrew his threat and didn't bring against his people the disaster he had threatened.
Exodus 32:7-14

* * *

"This is a test!" i don't know about you, but i like it better when i am told that at the onset! That way i know that everything i do and say is going to be weighed and evaluated for its correctness. i must confess i don't do as well when i don't think anyone is watching me or listening to me or evaluating me. But there is a lot to be learned through those surprise tests. When we take a test, it helps us measure how well we have learned what we have been taught and how well we have applied that learning. A test is a useful tool for a teacher to evaluate not only how well a student has learned, but also how well the teacher has taught. God will only allow us to be tested on that which He has taught us well. We can always be certain that He will not test us on anything that has not been "covered in class". And however God tests us, in His sovereignty He already knows what the outcome will be. The test is not for His benefit; it is for ours.

That day the people failed miserably. They had chosen to disobey God and disregard His Law. They had chosen to go their own way. They, who had trembled in fear before God just before Moses climbed the mountain, now danced before a golden calf, proclaiming it to be god. And God had promised that He would punish those who worshipped any other god.

Then God told Moses, "The people <u>you</u> brought from Egypt have defiled themselves. I will destroy them all, and I will make <u>you</u>, Moses, into a great nation." How would you have responded if you were Moses? Here was an opportunity for him to be not only the leader of the people, but to be a second Abraham - the father of the people. Jehovah would now be known as the God of Abraham, Isaac, Jacob <u>and Moses</u>. These people had grumbled and complained their way across the wilderness. They had threatened to kill Moses. This was an opportunity to be rid of their aggravation once and for all. It was an opportunity to become a patriarch of a new people – <u>the</u> people of God. What would you have said? "Okay, God, whatever You say?" Or "Yes, God, they deserve it; turn them into toast?"

You need to know – this is a test! This was as much a test for Moses as it was for the people. The people had failed, and now it was Moses' turn. How would Moses respond? Would he intercede for the people? Would he plead for them? God had called him to be their undershepherd – not only when they were obedient, but at all times. Their disobedience did not change his calling from God.

Let's step back and recap what we know about God's character. God is omniscient – He knows all things, even before they occur. God is the God of Truth and He will not violate His Word – what God promises, He fulfills. God knew the day He promised Abraham that these people would dishonor Him in this way on this day. But His promise to Abraham was not predicated on the people's integrity, it was predicated on God's – and God is not a man that He should lie. No, God would not utterly destroy this people that day; He would punish them, but He could not utterly destroy them because to do so would be to violate His Word. So what was this about? God had just given Moses the details to construct a wilderness tabernacle – God's dwelling place among His people. He had given Moses knowledge and now He was giving Moses the opportunity to demonstrate that he had a heart to go with that knowledge – a heart that first and foremost loved God and a heart that loved God's people. God could use a Moses who could demonstrate that kind of love to build His tabernacle and continue to lead His people.

As the psalmist wrote, God will test our thoughts and examine our hearts (Psa 17:3). No, God didn't change His mind that day, but Moses' faith was tested and found to be strong and pure (1 Pet 1:7). He passed the test. Remember, as you journey in this wilderness, that God will test you and prove you so that you too are ready for what lies ahead in your path (Jas 1:3-4).

* * *

50

THE DAY THE TABLETS SHATTERED

And when He had finished speaking with him upon Mount Sinai, He gave Moses the two tablets of the testimony, tablets of stone, written by the finger of God. Then Moses turned and went down the mountain. He held in his hands the two stone tablets inscribed with the terms of the covenant. They were inscribed on both sides, front and back. These stone tablets were God's work; the words on them were written by God himself. When they came near the camp, Moses saw the calf and the dancing. In terrible anger, he threw the stone tablets to the ground, smashing them at the foot of the mountain.
Exodus 31:18; 32:15-16, 19

* * *

God had given His people His Law. God had not only spoken it; He had written it with His finger on stone tablets. He had given the people His Law so that they would know how to love Him, how to live before Him, how to honor Him and how to love and honor one another. He was now giving them these stone tablets so they would know how much He loved them, and that He had called them to be His people and He would be their God. The Law, as it was obeyed, would be the people's covenant with God; the tablets were to be a constant reminder of God's covenant with His people. As the people obeyed the Law they would be expressing their love for God; as they looked at the tablets they would be reminded of the love God was expressing toward them. Jesus told His disciples, *"If you love Me, keep my commandments"* (John 14:15). But He also said, *"When you obey Me, you remain in My love"* (John 15:10). The first pointed to the responsibility of the people; the second to the promise of

God. The Law pointed to the responsibility of the people; the tablets pointed to the promise of God.

When the people came to Aaron with their gold and demanded that he make a golden idol that they could worship, they were willfully disobeying God's first and second commandment. But also through their disobedience they were in essence saying, "God, we do not love You. We do not desire for You to be our God. We do not desire to be Your people." Because if they truly loved God, they would keep His commandments, just as Jesus said. The same holds true for us. When we disobey God, we are not only sinning through our action of omission or commission, we are in fact saying to God, "God, I do not love you. I do not desire for you to be my God and I do not desire to be your child." Now very few of us would actually say that to God, but His Word tells us that we are saying just that through our acts of disobedience.

The people trashed the Law through their action that day, and in essence they trashed God's love. So i can't help but think that it was appropriate that the tablets were trashed that day as well. If the tablets were to be a reminder to the people of God's promise to love them as they obeyed Him, and their disobedience that day was an expression that they did not love God, isn't it fitting that God's reminder to them should be shattered?

Now you and i have a written revelation of God, His Truth and His promise; inspired by the Holy Spirit and written through men. God has given us His Word in the Person of His Son and through the inspiration of His Spirit in the Holy Scripture. But on that day, God had not only given His Word, He had written it with His own finger. And through the disobedience of His people the essence of His Word (the Law) was shattered, and the manifestation of His Word (the tablets) was also shattered. It is a visual reminder to us that when we disobey God's Word, we invalidate His promises to us. Our sin not only separates us from God, it separates us from His promises. Jesus said, *"If you stay joined to Me..., you may ask any request you like, and it will be granted"* (John 15:7). The shattering of the tablets demonstrates that we can no longer be assured of answered prayer, when we are disjoined from God through our disobedience (the breaking of the Law). Now let me hurriedly point out that we are not justified to God through the Law, but by faith in Christ Jesus (Gal 2:16-17). But Jesus tells us that if we are going to abide in His grace that we will obey His commands – that we cannot continue in unconfessed sin. If we remain in unconfessed sin, we have in essence shattered the tablets and broken covenant with God.

As you journey through the wilderness, and beyond, God has assured you of His presence, His promise and His love. But have you allowed the tablets of His promise to remain shattered in your life by allowing uncon-fessed sin to remain? God can and will restore that promise; He can put the shattered tablets back together again if you will let Him. The apostle John wrote, *"If we confess our sins to Him, He is faithful and just to forgive us and to cleanse us from every wrong"* (1 John 1:9).

Yes, the tablets shattered that day; but if the tablets are shattered in your life today, this is the day they can be restored.

* * *

51

THE AFTERMATH OF DISOBEDIENCE

When they came near the camp, Moses saw the calf and the dancing.... He took
the calf they had made and melted it in the fire. And when the metal had cooled, he
ground it into powder and mixed it with water. Then he made the people drink it.
...He stood at the entrance to the camp and shouted, "All of you who are on the
LORD's side, come over here and join me." And all the Levites came. He told
them, "This is what the LORD, the God of Israel, says: Strap on your swords! Go
back and forth from one end of the camp to the other, killing even your brothers,
friends, and neighbors." The Levites obeyed Moses, and about three thousand
people died that day. ...And the LORD sent a great plague upon the people
because they had worshiped the calf Aaron had made.
Exodus 32:19-20, 26-28, 35

* * *

The people had arisen early. The golden calf that Aaron had formed
stood in their midst. They had sat around it to eat and to drink. They
had risen to play around it. They bowed to it. They brought offerings to it
of every kind. They laughed, they sang and they danced around it. The
calf was bright and shiny; it was golden. Some of the people remarked
that they had never enjoyed this much pleasure. There were even some
scattered around the camp, some who had been against forming this
golden idol, who now found themselves being drawn into the celebration
by the euphoria of the crowd. They hadn't set out to disobey God, but
they were lured by the excitement and the appearance of pleasure. As the
day continued and the noise became more feverish and the activity more
frenzied, the people became more and more blinded to their disobedience.

That which had begun as deception had escalated to debauchery. But isn't that what sin does? It starts out as a deception – "God didn't really mean that" – or – "God won't mind if we do that just once" – or – "Who is it going to hurt?" Then we see the pleasure to be enjoyed and the fun to be experienced, and we want more. Let's face it, at its outset sin looks pleasurable. If it wasn't, we would never be tempted. But what we lose sight of is the cost of sin. And the insatiable thirst that develops for more and more. We are blinded to its price and to its cost until we are confronted with the aftermath of our disobedience.

The Israelites were dancing in their pleasure when Moses and Joshua arrived in the camp. And all of a sudden it was as if someone had turned on the light, and what they were enjoying in the darkness, now embarrassed and revolted them in the light. People began to scatter and distance themselves from their sin. Others looked around to see whom they could blame for their sin. A few in the group started to come up with excuses to justify their sin. Some tried to deny that they had any involvement in their sin. But most of the people just stood there feeling ashamed in their sin.

Moses took the calf that had been made in the fire and destroyed it in the fire. Then he ground it into powder and mixed the powder in the water for all the people to drink. He took the water that was sweet and made it bitter with the powder. God had taken bitter waters and made them sweet for this people, and now their sin had made sweet waters bitter. The first consequence that the people experienced in the aftermath of their disobedience was the bitter taste that sin will ultimately bring.

Then Moses called upon the Levites to put to death by the sword those who had led in this rebellion against God. We read that three thousand people died that day. Lest we be confused that was but a small number of the people who had worshipped the calf; these were those who had led in the rebellion. These experienced the temporal consequences for their sin. They experienced the physical pain – in their case, the sting of death – that is a part of the aftermath of disobedience. And notice Moses' instructions – none were to be spared, whether they be family, friend or neighbor. Sin is no respecter of persons. Its temporal price must be paid and it will be paid. It is a part of the aftermath of disobedience.

Then God took matters into His own hands. We read that God sent a great plague upon the people. Though we are not given an account, more than likely many died as a result, and many may have wished they would die. Some survived it, but were left with after effects as a constant reminder. They experienced the divine consequence for their disobedience. And though Scripture is silent on this account, based upon what we know about the character of God, i believe this consequence was directly affected by the condition of their heart in response to their disobedience. Some of the people were truly repentant before God and sought His cleansing and His forgiveness. Some of the people were merely remorseful before God and sought a second chance. Some of the people were stiff-necked before God and sought neither forgiveness nor grace. How do I know that? Because they were people like you and i, and that is how we respond – we respond either with repentance, unrepentant remorse or stiff-necked impenitence.

The remaining consequence in the aftermath of disobedience is the eternal consequence. And God tells us that the wages of sin is death. The eternal consequence of sin is eternal death, eternal separation from God – eternal damnation. But God alone has made a way for us to escape the eternal consequence for our sin through His Son, if we will but repent of our sin and surrender our lives to Him.

As you proceed on your journey, remember the lesson of the golden calf – turn from your sin and escape the aftermath of disobedience.

* * *

52

AND OUT CAME THIS CALF!

*After that, he turned to Aaron. "What did the people do to you?" he demanded.
"How did they ever make you bring such terrible sin upon them?" "Don't get
upset, sir," Aaron replied. "You yourself know these people and what a wicked
bunch they are. They said to me, 'Make us some gods to lead us, for something has
happened to this man Moses, who led us out of Egypt.' So I told them, 'Bring me
your gold earrings.' When they brought them to me, I threw them into the fire--
and out came this calf!" When Moses saw that Aaron had let the people get
completely out of control--and much to the amusement of their enemies--he stood
at the entrance to the camp and shouted, "All of you who are on the LORD's side,
come over here and join me." And all the Levites came. He told them, "This is
what the LORD, the God of Israel, says: Strap on your swords! Go back and forth
from one end of the camp to the other, killing even your brothers, friends, and
neighbors." The Levites obeyed Moses, and about three thousand people died that
day. ...And the LORD sent a great plague upon the people because they had
worshiped the calf Aaron had made.*
Exodus 32:21-28, 35

* * *

A lot of people died due to their disobedience in making and
worshipping the golden calf. They either were killed at the hands of
the Levites or died as a result of the plague. Even more suffered from the
plague as a result. The generations that followed were affected by this sin
of their parents. And yet, Scripture is silent regarding the consequences
that Aaron and Hur experienced for their sin – or is it? A casual reading

might lead us to believe that Aaron got little more than his hand slapped; but let's look further.

God does not grade on the curve. There is no hierarchy of sin. He tells us that the wages of sin – all sin and any sin – is death (Rom 6:23). He will not "pass us" on into heaven if we only sin certain sins and avoid the "biggies". The fact-of-the-matter is we are all sinners and have all fallen short of the glory of God (Rom 3:23). We are not sinners because we sin; we sin because we are sinners. Aaron and Hur were sinners just like you and me. Aaron and Hur were sinners that God, by His grace, elevated to a position of leadership among His people. They did not earn the position, God called them to it. God gave them authority as spiritual leaders over the people, but with that authority came responsibility and accountability.

Look at what Moses says to Aaron. "You have brought a terrible sin upon the people. What did these people do to you to make you do that?" Now each child of Israel was also a sinner; and each one was responsible for their own sin, but if the tribe turned to worship a golden calf then those leading the tribe – Aaron and Hur – had responsibility not only for their own choice, but also for their role in leading the tribe in this abomination, or their failure to lead the tribe away from it. And when confronted by Moses, Aaron gave the two classic excuses, "The people made me do it" and "I threw the gold in the fire – and out came this calf" (in other words, "I didn't do it, it just happened"). At that point, he denied any responsibility for his sin. He laid the blame at the feet of other people or circumstances "outside of his control". Have you ever done that? Have you ever tried to justify and deny your sin? God will not be deceived and He will not be mocked!

And we read here that because Aaron had let the people get completely out of control, they had become a laughing stock to their enemies. They had defamed their own name, but more critically they had dishonored the Name of their God. Three thousand died that day as a result of their sin and many more died, or at a minimum suffered, due to the plague that God sent because of the calf Aaron made.

The price of Aaron's disobedience was not his own death, rather it was living with the knowledge that his sin had led to the death of thousands – not the heroic death of a battle of honor, but a sinner's death resulting from the sin of dishonor. He also lived with the knowledge that generations to come would bear the scars of his disobedience. Moses writes, *"The LORD was so angry with Aaron that he wanted to destroy him. But I prayed for Aaron, and the LORD spared him"* (Deut 9:20 NLT). Because of Moses' intercession on his behalf, and in God's sovereign plan, God chose to spare Aaron's physical life, but He did not spare him from the consequence of the grief and anguish that he was forced to endure for forty years.

When Moses and Joshua climbed the mountain, Moses had left Aaron and Hur in charge of the people. This is the last time we read of Hur in Scripture. Hereafter we only see his name in lists of ancestry. We never read that he opposed the making of the calf. If Hur had honored God by opposing this abomination, it would have been recorded in Scripture. No mention is made whether he stood silently by and did not protest, whether he led in the rebellion, or whether like Aaron, he went along with the people. Regardless of which action he took, the absence of his presence hereafter causes me to think Hur died for his disobedience that day, either by the sword or due to the plague. Remember, Hur was Moses' brother-in-law; he was Miriam's husband. And as Moses instructed the Levites as they strapped on their swords, God is not a respecter of persons when it comes to sin. i would conjecture that God chose not to spare Hur's physical life.

Which one paid the greater price for their disobedience – Aaron enduring forty years of grief and anguish, or Hur experiencing physical death? i'll leave that to you to decide. But as you journey through the wilderness, God has placed you in a role to encourage and to lead others; with that role comes responsibility and accountability. Not only has He called you to obey Him, He has called you to lead others to obey Him. Heed that call. That is part of His reason for placing you on this journey. At the end of the day, it doesn't matter if Aaron formed the calf or if it "just came out". The result was the same, and the consequence was great. Heed the call. Honor the Lord – and lead His people to do so as well.

* * *

53

DON'T GO WITHOUT HIM

*The LORD said to Moses, "Now that you have brought these people out of Egypt,
lead them to the land I solemnly promised Abraham, Isaac, and Jacob. I told them
long ago that I would give this land to their descendants. And I will send an angel
before you to drive out the Canaanites, Amorites, Hittites, Perizzites, Hivites, and
Jebusites. Theirs is a land flowing with milk and honey. But I will not travel along
with you, for you are a stubborn, unruly people. If I did, I would be tempted to
destroy you along the way." Then Moses said, "If you don't go with us
personally, don't let us move a step from this place. If you don't go with us, how
will anyone ever know that your people and I have found favor with you? How
else will they know we are special and distinct from all other people on the earth?"
And the LORD replied to Moses, "I will indeed do what you have asked, for you
have found favor with me, and you are my friend."*
Exodus 33:1-3, 15-17

* * *

At the burning bush, God had said He would bring His people to the
land flowing with milk and honey (Ex 3). Then when He brought
Moses back to Sinai with the people, God had again promised to send His
Spirit before the people and bring them into the land (Ex 23). But now,
after the people had turned from God and worshipped the golden calf,
God said He would not go with them or before them; He would send an
angel. The people's disobedience had not only cost them the wrath of
God, it was now costing them the absence of His presence. Though God
told Moses that He would keep His promise to Abraham, Isaac and Jacob
and that this people would experience the blessing of God; they would not

experience His presence. This was a stubborn and unruly and ungrateful people, and though their sin would not cost them the blessings of God's provision it would cost them the blessings of His presence.

But Moses knew that no matter how great things might be in the Promised Land, it would mean nothing without God's presence.

Today as you journey through the wilderness, you may be at a place where you are desperate for God's provision, protection or power. You may find yourself longing for that Promised Land, that land flowing with milk and honey. You may find yourself spent from the journey, with all of your resources and strength spent. You have experienced God's blessings along the way, but you are tired and you are ready to be there. Nothing ever looked as good as that Promised Land does right now. Be careful, it is during times like these that we can become so focused on God's provision that we stop watching for His presence. We can be so focused on God's hands of blessing that we forget the warmth of His presence.

Moses interceded, "LORD, if you don't go with us, don't let us take another step." Their journey was all about God, and the glory of His Name. If He didn't go with them, how would a watching world know that they were His people? The blessing that differentiated them as a people was not the blessing of His provision; it was the blessing of His presence.

God has blessed our nation with tremendous wealth. The American church enjoys tremendous financial blessing compared to the body of Christ throughout the rest of the world. And yet for all of our buildings and budgets, what is it about us that causes the world to see a difference in us? It will never be the blessings of God's provision; it must be the blessing of His obvious presence. The world is blind to our financial prosperity, but when God's presence becomes conspicuous the world takes notice. And that condition is not limited to our churches, that statement is true in our homes and in our lives personally. If those around us are not seeing that difference, is it because we have settled for God's provision and gone ahead without His presence?

Must we, like Moses, come to that place that we turn to God and declare, "LORD, if you don't go with us, don't let us take another step." Do not bless us at all if that blessing comes without the benefit of Your presence.

Would we be willing to have all of our blessings stripped away, provided we were assured that God's presence would remain with us? Do we long for Him and His presence that much? Do we desire <u>Him</u> that much – and not the "things" that He provides? That is the kind of love He has for us and desires for us to have for Him. i believe it was that kind of love that Paul spoke of when he said that he had learned how to be content whether he was abased or abound. It is a joy and a peace and a contentment that only comes through the presence of the Living Lord.

My prayer is that as we journey through the wilderness each of us would long for His presence above all else; and that we too would come to Him with the resolve that says, "We won't go without You".

* * *

54

BUT MOSES WANTED MORE

And the LORD replied to Moses, "I will indeed do what you have asked, for you have found favor with me, and you are my friend." Then Moses had one more request. "Please let me see your glorious presence," he said. The LORD replied, "I will make all my goodness pass before you, and I will call out my name, 'the LORD,' to you. I will show kindness to anyone I choose, and I will show mercy to anyone I choose. But you may not look directly at my face, for no one may see me and live." The LORD continued, "Stand here on this rock beside me. As my glorious presence passes by, I will put you in the cleft of the rock and cover you with my hand until I have passed. Then I will remove my hand, and you will see me from behind. But my face will not be seen."
Exodus 33:17-23

* * *

M oses had already experienced an intimacy with the Lord God Jehovah that exceeded that which most men have ever experienced this side of heaven. God had called Moses His friend - a designation that to this point had only been shared with Abraham. Moses had found favor with God; His actions had demonstrated a heart that desired to seek and serve his Lord. He spoke to God with a confidence and a boldness that also conveyed reverence and awe. God had used Moses as His chosen vessel when He turned the water into blood, the bitter into sweet, and the Red Sea into an instrument of deliverance and destruction. God had taken a man who worried about his eloquence before Pharaoh and given him a boldness of speech before the God of heaven. God had taken a shepherd from the mountains of Horeb and made him into His undershepherd over

His flock. God had chosen to meet with Moses at a burning bush, in the Tent of meeting, and on Mount Sinai in the clouds. God had given him immediate access to His throne when he called upon Him for wisdom, direction and deliverance. But Moses wanted more! He had heard God's voice, and He had experienced God's presence, but that caused Him to desire to see God's glory – not from afar, but close up.

The more time we spend with God, the more time we will desire to spend with Him. The more we hear His voice, the more we will desire to hear Him. The more we experience His presence, the more we will desire to experience Him. The closer we draw to His presence, the closer still we will desire to be. The more we know Him, the more we will love Him. The more we love Him, the closer we will desire to be to Him. The closer we draw to Him the more we will know Him, and the more we will desire to see of Him. Spending time in the presence of God will place within our souls an insatiable thirst to spend more time with God. i have heard people ask, "What will we be able to do in heaven for eternity?" We will be able to spend eternity with God! If that doesn't make sense to you then i would assert that you have not yet spent time in the intimacy of His presence. Too many of us are content to know about God or to know Him from a distance, just like the children of Israel did. But Moses desired to know Him more. He desired to be with Him even closer.

What about you? Do you desire to know Him more? Do you desire to see His glory? i don't mean a mental assent that says, "Of course, I am a Christian, that is what I am supposed to want." i'm talking about an insatiable heart hunger that cries out to God for more and more of Him. A cry that says, "I am not content to stand afar off with the crowd and see You. I desire to be in Your presence and look upon You."

Throughout God's Word He has promised that if we seek Him with our whole hearts, we will find Him. God made the Way through His Son that we might know Him and that we might know the intimacy of His presence. He gave us the thirst to be in His presence. Unfortunately we, even we who claim to be God's children, have allowed other things – counterfeits – to try to satisfy that thirst; and we have done it for so long that we can no longer tell the difference. But God desires to change that in our lives. If we will surrender to Him whatever we have allowed to be that substitute, He will replace it with the real thing. He will give us that desire – and that desire for more.

Through Jesus we have been allowed access to an elite fellowship with God. Jesus has told us, *"You are My friends if you obey Me. I no longer call you servants, because a master doesn't confide in his servants. Now you are My friends, since I have told you everything the Father told Me* (John 15:14-15) He has called us His friend. He has given us the same access that Abraham and Moses had, if we will but obey Him. And with that access comes the right, honor and privilege of knowing Him more.

God covered Moses with His hand until He had passed, because he knew that Moses could not see His glory in its fullness and live. But God granted His request; He enabled Moses to see His glorious presence from behind. And as he saw, he wanted still more.

God has led you on this journey through the wilderness so that through it, you might know Him, know Him more and know Him more intimately. Respond to His invitation to know Him and you too, will want even more.

* * *

55

STARTING OVER

The LORD told Moses, "Prepare two stone tablets like the first ones. I will write on them the same words that were on the tablets you smashed. Be ready in the morning to come up Mount Sinai and present yourself to me there on the top of the mountain. No one else may come with you. In fact, no one is allowed anywhere on the mountain. Do not even let the flocks or herds graze near the mountain." So Moses cut two tablets of stone like the first ones. Early in the morning he climbed Mount Sinai as the LORD had told him, carrying the two stone tablets in his hands.
Exodus 34:1-4

* * *

The tablets that God had prepared as a tangible expression of His covenant with His people had made their way down the mountain, but never made their way to the people. As the people stood there worshiping that golden calf, their sin caused those tablets to be destroyed. Their sin kept them from receiving that blessing from the Lord. But now the people had been punished for their sin. They had turned in repentance back to God. Moses had interceded for the people; God had promised to continue to go before His people. Everything was back to the way it was just before the people sinned – right? When we sin and then turn back to God in repentance, receiving His cleansing and forgiveness, everything goes back to just like it was at the moment before we sinned - doesn't it? Doesn't God bring us right back to the place that we were? Doesn't our relationship with Him pick right back up from where we were? Don't we return to the very spot we were before we sinned?

God in essence was saying to Moses here, "We're starting over. Prepare two stone tablets *like* the first ones." The people would never have those original tablets again. God instructed Moses to prepare tablets that were "like" the first ones; they would be similar, but they would not be the originals. You may recall that God supplied the original tablets. No human hand had formed them; God Himself had prepared the original tablets. Now Moses was preparing this replacement set. They would be very similar in appearance. They would be like the originals in size and shape and material, but they would never be the originals. The sin of the people had caused them to miss out on God's best – His original. The best they could now ever hope to experience was His replica, His second best. They couldn't return to the exact same place they were before. God would bring them back, but it would never be as if they had never sinned to begin with; it would be similar, but it would never be what He had originally given them.

i am reminded of the sin of Adam and Eve. When they repented, God forgave them, but their lives – and ours – never returned to what they were prior to their sin. They had to start over – in a new place (no longer in the garden), in a new way (now clothed with the skin of animals), and in a new relationship (no longer walking with Him in the garden in the cool of the day). It is a testimony to God's grace that he made a way for Adam and Eve to start over, and that He told the people through Moses to make preparations to start over.

At this point, i'm hearing the question, "Well if I can't go back to where I was, then why should I even try to start over?" **Because God's second best will always be far greater than anything that we or this world have to offer.** Yes, the reality is, our sin has caused us to no longer experience God's absolute best, but He has made a way for us to start over. And though, while we are in this world what we will experience will never be as great as if we had not sinned to begin with, it will be far greater than we deserve and far greater than we can imagine. And when we leave this world, if we are a follower of Jesus, we will spend eternity with Him in a place that is His absolute best – a place where there is no sin and there never has been any; and we will leave all the baggage of the sin of our lives and of this world behind.

If we are going to start over, we, like Moses, must prepare the tablets and present ourselves. The tablets were where God was going to inscribe His Word. God desires to inscribe His Word on our hearts. We must prepare our hearts. Our hearts must be cleansed and softened so that there is nothing to prevent us from receiving God's Word. Our hearts must be moldable and responsive so that we can respond to God's Word. And we must present our bodies. Paul wrote, "Present your bodies a living and holy sacrifice, acceptable to God, which is your spiritual service of worship" (Rom 12:1 NAS). We must surrender all of ourselves, making whatever adjustment God calls us to make.

God told Moses to cut out the tablets and climb the mountain. If God is calling you to start over in this journey, then prepare your heart by extricating it from the things of this world that entangle it and allow Him to lead you into the place of His presence. It is in that place that He will begin His work in you of starting over.

* * *

56

GOD PASSED BY

*The LORD replied, "I will make all my goodness pass before you, and I will call
out my name, 'the LORD,' to you. ...Early in the morning he climbed Mount
Sinai as the LORD had told him, carrying the two stone tablets in his hands.
Then the LORD came down in a pillar of cloud and called out his own name, "the
LORD," as Moses stood there in his presence. He passed in front of Moses and
said, "I am the LORD, I am the LORD, the merciful and gracious God. I am slow
to anger and rich in unfailing love and faithfulness. I show this unfailing love to
many thousands by forgiving every kind of sin and rebellion. Even so I do not
leave sin unpunished, but I punish the children for the sins of their parents to the
third and fourth generations." Moses immediately fell to the ground and
worshiped.*
Exodus 33:19; 34:4-8

* * *

In the wilderness, there are some things God will only teach you once
He gets you alone with Himself. Moses had climbed Mount Sinai and
stood alone in God's presence several times before. While standing there,
Moses had heard God's plan to deliver His people (Ex 3), God's exacting
boundaries (Ex 19), and God's instructions for the building of the tabernacle (Ex 24 – 31). And on this day, Moses again climbed the mountain to
stand in God's presence.

Let me take a quick side road here. In order for you and me to enter into
the presence of God, we must leave where we are and "step up" into His

presence; and it requires God to move from where He is and "step down" in order to allow us to step into His presence. God in His compassion will humble Himself and come to us. (The ultimate picture of this compassion and humility – this "stepping down" – is Jesus coming to earth as the Son of Man, that we might see Him and know Him.)

As Moses stood there, God passed by; and as He passed, He declared His Name. He declared Himself to be Jehovah, the I Am, full of mercy, full of grace, longsuffering, and abounding in lovingkindness and truth. He declared His love for all and His forgiveness of the repentant; but He declared that He is just and will by no means leave the guilty unpunished. And as His goodness and His glory passed before Moses, there was only one response that Moses could give – he fell to the ground and worshipped God. Moses stood no more. Moses himself tells us, *"Then for forty days and nights I lay prostrate before the LORD, neither eating bread nor drinking water"* (Deut 9:18).

Do you want to know if you have ever stood in God's presence? If you're not sure, you probably haven't. When God visits His presence upon us, we will not stand on ceremony, we will not stand at all; we will bow in worship. When God passes by, He will reveal His Name, His glory and His goodness. We will not be concerned about our time, our business or our agendas; we will lay prostrate at His feet.

Why did Moses alone experience God in this way? Why were the rest of the people not invited? Why was only Moses able to see God when He passed by?

First, God chose Moses. It was God who first seized Moses' attention through a bush that burned without being consumed. It was God that spoke to him when he turned his attention to God. Paul writes that the Father chose us in Christ before the foundation of the world (Eph 1:4). We have been chosen by God to enter into a relationship with Him. We can only come to Him because He has first chosen us. Jesus taught, *"No one can come to Me unless the Father who sent Me draws him"* (John 6:44) and *"No one comes to the Father except through Me"* (John 14:6). We are His because He chose us. We can come to Him because He chose us. He has chosen us to be His child and to experience His Person and His presence.

Second, Moses obeyed God. When God extended His invitation to Moses to climb the mountain, Moses did not hesitate. He made whatever adjustment was necessary, leaving all else behind, to enter into the presence of God. He left his wife, his children, his possessions and his responsibilities and climbed the mountain. Now some people might have called him irresponsible to do such a thing, and apart from an invitation from God, they would be right. But when God invites you, allowing your responsibilities to get in the way of your obedience is sin. The key is knowing God's voice. Moses didn't need to ask God if that was His voice. Moses knew God's voice, through spending time with Him. We too will know His voice as we spend time with Him.

Third, Moses sought God. God allowed Moses to see His glory because he asked to see God's glory. Most of us are not seeing God's glory because we are not seeking His glory. We are like the multitude that day; we have become satisfied with the view we have of God from where we are at the base of the mountain. James wrote that we don't have, because we don't ask (James 4:2).

If you are a child of God, He desires to reveal His glory in you, to you and through you. You are His child because He has chosen you. He has set your feet on this journey for that purpose. If you will obey Him and respond to His voice; and if you will seek Him with your whole heart, He will be found by you. You will enter into His presence, and the glory of His presence will pass by. And you will respond in the only way you can – you will fall to the ground and worship Him.

* * *

57

LET HIS LIGHT SHINE

The LORD replied, "All right. This is the covenant I am going to make with you.
I will perform wonders that have never been done before anywhere in all the earth
or in any nation. And all the people around you will see the power of the LORD--
the awesome power I will display through you. Moses was up on the mountain
with the LORD forty days and forty nights.... When Moses came down the
mountain.., he wasn't aware that his face glowed because he had spoken to the
LORD face to face. And when Aaron and the people of Israel saw the radiance of
Moses' face, they were afraid to come near him. But Moses called to them and
asked Aaron and the community leaders to come over and talk with him. Then all
the people came, and Moses gave them the instructions the LORD had given him
on Mount Sinai. When Moses had finished speaking with them, he put a veil over
his face.
Exodus 34:10, 28-33

* * *

Moses spent forty days and nights on the mountain, prostrate before the Lord, basking in His glory. God promised him that He would perform wonders that had never been seen, and all the people of the world would see His awesome power displayed through His people. God rewrote His covenant with the people on the stone tablets and renewed His commitment to go before the people. But as Moses descended the mountain, it was not the tablets that he carried that drew the attention of the people, it was his face.

It was conspicuous that Moses had been with God. The Shekinah glory of God's presence radiated from his face. It was obvious that he had spent time with God, not only by his actions and his words, but also by his appearance.

Moses didn't realize that his face shone. It wasn't a work of his own hand; it was a work that God had done from the inside out. It was a by-product of the deeper work that God had done in his life. Man may attempt to make changes on the outside that indicate a change on the inside, but they will pale and they will point to ourselves. God's work will remain and reveal His handiwork. Moses face shined as brightly as the noonday sun but it wasn't a radiated light, it was a reflected light. The light did not originate with Moses; it originated with God. But as Moses spent time with God, God shaped him into a vessel through whom His glory could be reflected. Paul wrote, *"So that we can be mirrors that brightly reflect the glory of the Lord. And as the Spirit of the Lord works within us, we become more and more like Him and reflect His glory even more"* (2 Cor 3:18).

The people were afraid to come near Moses. It wasn't that they didn't know who he was or even why his face was shining; it was that they didn't know how to respond. God's holiness demands reverence and awe. The people were struck with awe, not of Moses, but of God; but they no longer knew how to act around Moses. Then Moses called them over and told them all that God had instructed him on the mount. This time because of the glory that they saw, they received God's instruction with that same reverence and awe. (If that is true, could it be that the people around us do not receive God's instruction from us because they don't see His glory reflected through us?)

After Moses spoke, he humbly covered his face so as not to bring attention to himself. Moses reflected the same Christlike attitude of which Paul writes when he says, *"Your attitude should be the same that Christ Jesus had. Though He was God, He did not demand and cling to His rights as God. He made Himself nothing; He took the humble position of a slave"* (Phil 2:5-7). Moses would have nothing that drew attention to himself and away from his Lord.

Having sought God's glory, Moses had now experienced God's glory, and the result was that:

- God's glory was humbly revealed by God's man who fell down in worship,
- God's glory was humbly revered by God's people who stood back in awe and
- God's glory was humbly concealed by God's man who walked forth in service.

God desires for us to enter into His presence and to experience His glory. He is removing the dross from our lives so that His glory might be reflected through us. He desires to reveal His glory through a people that are wholly committed and available to be used by Him. If His glory is not shining on our faces, perhaps it is because we have not entered into His presence. i don't mean the routine of a quiet time; i mean having sought Him and His glory, we experience the presence of His Person. If His Light is to shine through our lives, it will first be reflected on our faces. That is why He has us on this journey. Let His Light shine!

* * *

58

ONLY IF YOU ARE WILLING

Then Moses said to all the people, "This is what the LORD has commanded.
Everyone is invited to bring these offerings to the LORD.... So all the people left
Moses and went to their tents to prepare their gifts. If their hearts were stirred
and they desired to do so, they brought to the LORD their offerings of materials
for the Tabernacle and its furnishings and for the holy garments. Both men and
women came, all whose hearts were willing.... So the people of Israel -- every man
and woman who wanted to help in the work the LORD had given them through
Moses -- brought their offerings to the LORD.
Exodus 35:4-5, 20-22, 29

* * *

They were preparing to build the tabernacle – the earthly dwelling
place of God among His people! God had given very specific
instructions in how the tabernacle and all of its furnishings were to be
constructed. Everything would be built according to His plan and His
specifications.

Though God had only just given these specifications to Moses, they were
in the mind of God that day at the burning bush when He instructed
Moses to tell the people, *"And I will see to it that the Egyptians treat you well.*
They will load you down with gifts so you will not leave empty-handed. The
Israelite women will ask for silver and gold jewelry and fine clothing from their
Egyptian neighbors and their neighbors' guests" (Ex 3:21-22). God had made
provision that every resource that was required to construct the tabernacle

was already in the possession of the Israelites. God had provided it through the Egyptians and entrusted it to the Israelites to carry. God had provided it for His purpose.

Now was the time for the resources to be assembled. Moses announced, "Everyone is invited to bring their offerings to the Lord." It is interesting to note that Moses did not say, "Everyone is commanded to bring." They were expressly told that they were only to give an offering if they desired to do so and their hearts were willing. Only those who wanted to help in the work were to bring an offering. This was to be a freewill offering – freely returning to God that which He Himself had already provided for His purpose – the building of His tabernacle.

It is also interesting to note that this was a people on a journey through the wilderness. These were not wealthy people; they were servants and ex-slaves. These were not people with a steady source of income; these were a people without any current income. These were not landowners; they were sojourners. These were not people giving out of their surplus; they were giving out of their humble means. And yet God was giving them an opportunity to be a part of His work, if they so chose; and He had given them the resources to be able to do so.

Returning to God that which is His to begin with should be easy for us as His children to do, but all too often it is not. We clench His provision in our fists and declare it to be ours. We ignore His purpose for which He provided it and redirect it to our purpose for our comfort or our pleasure. We rob God of His provision, and rob ourselves of the joy of giving. Paul wrote, "You must each make up your own mind as to how much you should give. Don't give reluctantly or in response to pressure. For God loves the person who gives cheerfully. And God will generously provide all you need. Then you will always have everything you need and plenty left over to share with others" (2 Cor 9:7-8).

There were some in that group who had no part in the offering. They picked up God's manna every morning but would not bring a love offering to Him. They rationalized it. They tried to justify it. But the fact-of-the-matter was they just didn't love God enough – enough to give.

What about us? Do we love Him enough – enough to give? i am grateful that He loved me enough to give – enough to give His Son! And He gave Him willingly! He gave Jesus so that His eternal purpose could be accomplished – and that purpose included my salvation – the forgiveness of my sins. And my life and my heart have become His earthly dwelling place. He has included me in the Story of His glory! He has enabled me to be a part of His Story, and He has enabled me to participate in His Story using the time, talent and treasure He has entrusted me with. But only if i am willing.

God has entrusted you with resources for this journey through this wilderness. Do not hoard them. Give them to Him. But only if you are willing.

* * *

59
___

CALLED AND COMPETENT

And Moses told them, "The LORD has chosen Bezalel son of Uri, grandson of Hur, of the tribe of Judah. The LORD has filled Bezalel with the Spirit of God, giving him great wisdom, intelligence, and skill in all kinds of crafts. He is able to create beautiful objects from gold, silver, and bronze. He is skilled in cutting and setting gemstones and in carving wood. In fact, he has every necessary skill. And the LORD has given both him and Oholiab son of Ahisamach, of the tribe of Dan, the ability to teach their skills to others. The LORD has given them special skills as jewelers, designers, weavers, and embroiderers in blue, purple, and scarlet yarn on fine linen cloth. They excel in all the crafts needed for the work."
Exodus 35:30-35

* * *

God was leading His people to build His tabernacle, His earthly dwelling place among His people. He gave the detailed specifications for its construction. He provided for His people, and through His people, all of the materials that were required to construct it. And God had placed within their ranks the men that He had uniquely prepared for just this work.

God called them; He chose them and He set them apart. God called Bezalel to be the lead craftsmen, the lead builder. Bezalel had a unique parentage; he was the grandson of Hur and Miriam (Moses' sister). But more importantly, he had a unique preparation; he was filled by God with His Spirit. God had equipped him with every skill that would be necessary to complete the work. God had given him great wisdom, intelligence and skill. God called Oholiab to be Bezalel's assistant, having given him all of the necessary skill to accomplish his assignment. And God had given them both the ability to teach their skills to others.

Whenever God is leading His people to accomplish His task, He will call His person that He has appointed to lead through the completion of the task. Whenever you see God stirring among His people, you will see Him stirring the hearts of one man or woman, or a small group of men and women, to be His point-person(s) for that particular task. Their assignment is to lead God's people through the completion of the task, according to God's plan and specifications. It is interesting to note that God did not call Moses to this assignment. Though God had given Moses the detailed plan, He had selected another with the responsibility of leading the people in the completion of this task. And Moses demonstrated wisdom and discernment in letting go and allowing God to work in the way and through the people that He intended. God has an assignment for every one of His people; watch to see whom He has called, and be willing to step aside when He has called another.

Whomever God calls, He equips. It has been truly said that God does not always call the equipped, but He always equips the called. Those whom He has called, He has made competent. Bezalel's competency was not the result of his skill; his competency was the result of his calling of God and his filling by the Holy Spirit. The key issue then for Bezalel, as it is for each of us, was his availability and obedience to God's call, not his ability. God would give him the competency to complete all that was required. Some of that skill had been demonstrated through Bezalel's natural abilities over the years, but God completed and perfected those abilities through the presence and empowerment of His Holy Spirit.

Whomever God calls, He will equip with the ability to teach others. God's assignments are not solely for the few; God's assignments are for all of His people. The position of minister is not a profession for the select; it is to be the predisposition of all the saints. Therefore those that God calls into positions of leadership, He will equip to train and to teach others for the work of the ministry. God was preparing to build His earthly dwelling place among His people, and He was extending an invitation to all of His people – those who were willing – to be a part of carrying out His task.

Could God have supernaturally built His earthly dwelling place? Could He have spoken it into existence the same as He spoke the earth, the sun and the stars into existence? Did He need Bezalel and Oholiab and all of the people to accomplish this task? God has repeatedly demonstrated that He created us, He chose us, and if we name the Name of Jesus He saved us, so that He might accomplish His work through us to His glory. No, He doesn't need us; but He has chosen to use us. And those whom He has chosen, He has called. And those He has called, He has made competent. If we are followers of Christ, we are His workmanship. We are, in fact, His earthly tabernacle – His earthly dwelling place. He indwells our lives for the purpose of accomplishing His purpose that will lead to His glory. Those he indwells He will call; and those He calls He will make competent.

Even in the wilderness, God makes assignments, just as He did that day. What is God's assignment for you? Step out in obedience and in confidence – for you are called and competent!

* * *

60

MORE THAN ENOUGH

So Moses told Bezalel and Oholiab to begin the work, along with all those who were specially gifted by the LORD. Moses gave them the materials donated by the people for the completion of the sanctuary. Additional gifts were brought each morning. But finally the craftsmen left their work to meet with Moses. "We have more than enough materials on hand now to complete the job the LORD has given us to do!" they exclaimed. So Moses gave the command, and this message was sent throughout the camp: "Bring no more materials! You have already given more than enough." So the people stopped bringing their offerings. Their contributions were more than enough to complete the whole project.
Exodus 36:2-7

* * *

Just once i'd like to hear that proclaimed from a pulpit. Just once in my lifetime i would like to hear, "Bring no more. You have given more than enough." i'd like to hear that the offerings are more than enough to complete the task that God has given us – the whole project!

But why do we never hear that? Why are the church of our Lord Jesus Christ and the ministries of His body all too often dependent upon emotional offering appeals, fund raising campaigns and marketing tactics to raise needed financial resources? Is it because God hasn't provided those resources to His people as He did to the Israelites through the Egyptians? Is that the problem? Is it shortage of resources?

We live in a day and a society that has been blessed (or cursed, depending upon your perspective) with the greatest wealth of financial resources in history. God has prospered His people with an unprecedented reservoir of resources to accomplish His purpose and complete His task in this time. Within this generation, the great commission could be fulfilled. The Good News of the Gospel could be carried to every people, every tongue and every tribe throughout Jerusalem, Judea, Samaria and the remotest parts of the earth. The completion of that task in our day is as visible as the completion of the task of building His tabernacle was in that day. And just like then, God has provided everything that is necessary to complete His appointed task. So, why is no one saying, "Bring no more, you've given more than enough"?

Statistics gathered by the *Global Evangelization Movement* indicate members of churches in the United States give 1.7% of their income to all Christian causes. And though the percentage among evangelicals is slightly higher, still less than one out of every ten adult evangelical Christians tithes. So the problem does not appear to be shortage of resources that God has provided to His people, it appears to be our stewardship of those resources.

The Israelites had now been on their journey through the wilderness for approximately six months. Their grumbling, their complaining and their disobedience along the way had not demonstrated that their hearts were fully turned toward God. On the contrary they had repeatedly displayed a selfishness and a self-centeredness that rivals even that displayed in our day. So what was different, why did they willingly bring more than enough?

Do you remember what had happened approximately six weeks before this? They had willingly taken up an offering in disobedience to God for the image of the golden calf. How is it that we, like they, don't seem to have any hesitancy in spending our resources in ways that dishonor God? We will willingly spend our resources on things that bring us pleasure or pamper our egos, or even those things that take us further from God.

But following that act of disobedience, they experienced the discipline of God in a way that they never had before. They saw thousands of their number die both by the sword and as a result of the plague. And as they saw those around them experiencing the consequence of sin, they began to understand that though God was merciful, He was also just, and that He would *"by no means clear the guilty"* (Ex 34:7). But just as many of them experienced death or disease as a result of their sin, many of them received mercy. And they began to see the Lord God Jehovah through eyes of reverence and awe, with fear and with trembling. Walking in the fear of the Lord is walking in the awareness of His love, His grace and His mercy, but it is also walking in the awareness of His might, His power, His righteousness and His justness. As we walk in that awareness of who He is, we will begin to live our lives understanding that every thought, attitude and action is under His eye. Peter wrote, The Father *"will judge or reward you according to what you do. So you must live in reverent fear of Him during your time as foreigners here on earth"* (1 Peter 1:17).

They gave willingly because they feared God. That is not an oxymoron. They gave out of reverence for God. We do not give, because we have lost our reverence for God. We have become so focused toward His love, His grace and His mercy that we have used them as license to ignore His might, His power, His righteousness and His justness. When will we hear the proclamation from the pulpit, "Bring no more, you've given more than enough"? When we begin to give out of obedience to Him, love for Him, and reverence of Him. And i pray that we would not need to experience His discipline before we do so.

Perhaps as you journey through this wilderness, you have not yet experienced the joy of giving until the Lord says, "Bring no more, you've given more than enough." He's brought you here to teach you who He is. Respond to Him today, just like the Israelites did that day in the wilderness.

* * *

61

HIS DWELLING PLACE

And so at last the Tabernacle was finished. The Israelites had done everything just as the LORD had commanded Moses. ...So the Tabernacle was set up on the first day of the new year. ...Then the cloud covered the Tabernacle, and the glorious presence of the LORD filled it. Moses was no longer able to enter the Tabernacle because the cloud had settled down over it, and the Tabernacle was filled with the awesome glory of the LORD. Now whenever the cloud lifted from the Tabernacle and moved, the people of Israel would set out on their journey, following it. But if the cloud stayed, they would stay until it moved again. The cloud of the LORD rested on the Tabernacle during the day, and at night there was fire in the cloud so all the people of Israel could see it. This continued throughout all their journeys.
Exodus 39:32; 40:17, 34-38

* * *

On the first day of the second year after their departure from Egypt, the Tabernacle had now been finished and erected according to the Lord's specifications. The Lord's glorious presence had now descended upon it, covering it and filling it with His awesome glory. God's presence, as manifested by the pillar of cloud, had gone before them since the journey began, but on this day His presence entered and indwelt His dwelling place among them. And from that day forward throughout the rest of their journey, when His Spirit led, the people would continue on their journey; when His Spirit inhabited the Tabernacle, the people would encamp.

Though their journey was far from over, they had come to a place where, no matter where they were, they dwelt in the presence of God because He dwelt in their midst. They dwelt in the shelter of the Most High and in the shadow of the Almighty. A journey that had begun to escape the slavery of Egypt had become a journey into God's presence.

What was unique about this people that the Lord God Jehovah dwelt among them? Was it their obedience each and every step throughout their journey? No, because they had demonstrated themselves to be a stiff-necked disobedient people throughout the journey. Was it their faithfulness to worship Him and Him alone? No, because this same people, who had constructed the Tabernacle, had formed the image of the golden calf. Was it their walk of faith and their trust in Him? No, at each crossroad of faith they had demonstrated a faithlessness in the God Who's Spirit went before them, often ignoring and denying His presence. This people had done nothing to earn or to merit God's favor; they did not deserve to have the God of Heaven dwelling among them. He dwelt among them because He chose to do so. He chose them to be His people; they had not chosen Him to be their God. He promised to bless all the nations through this people; and He who had promised was faithful, even though they had broken every promise they had made to Him. He continued to demonstrate His love for His people, even when they were their most unlovely.

He dwelt among His people, because He chose them to be His people. Even though they were sinners, He chose them. Even though they were sinners, He loved them. Even though they were sinners, He led them. And even when they could not do anything to reconcile themselves to a Holy God, He made a way. Even when they did not grasp the desperateness of their condition, He made a way. Even when they turned against His Son, He made a way.

And He made a way for you and me – and His Name is Jesus. As we journey through this current wilderness, as well as the one that will undoubtedly follow if Jesus tarries in His return, God has invited us to walk in His Way; and if we walk in His Way, it is because He has chosen us. And if we are walking in His Way, we can walk with the confidence that He dwells within us. We dwell in the shelter of the Most High; we dwell in the shadow of the Almighty. The journey that we are on is His journey. He set our feet on the path. He set forth the path. He has determined the journey's end. He has a purpose for the journey. He will use the journey for our good – to conform us more into the image of His Son – and

He will use the journey for His glory. Be careful as you continue in the journey, our good and His glory will not solely be determined by our destination, He is using the journey itself. You are His Tabernacle – His dwelling place.

Those who live in the shelter of the Most High
will find rest in the shadow of the Almighty.
This I declare of the LORD:
He alone is my refuge, my place of safety;
he is my God, and I am trusting him.
For he will rescue you from every trap
and protect you from the fatal plague.
He will shield you with his wings.
He will shelter you with his feathers.
His faithful promises are your armor and protection.
Ps 91:1-4

Journey well, fellow sojourner. Heed this lesson learned in the wilderness. You are His dwelling place.

* * *

SIGN UP TO RECEIVE A FREE BOOK

i would like to send you a free copy of *The Journey Begins* e-book — this first book in the *Lessons Learned In The Wilderness* series. It is yours to keep or share with a friend or family member that you think might benefit from it.

In addition, you'll be added to my Readers' Group and will be the first to hear about updates and future releases in the series.

It's completely free to sign up. i value your privacy and will not spam you. Also, you can unsubscribe at any time.

Go to www.kenwinter.org to subscribe.

* * *

PLEASE LEAVE A REVIEW!

If you have found this book to be helpful, i would be honored if you would leave a review.

Your review can help other readers in their decision-making to pick up a copy of this book as well.

To leave a review, go to:
amazon.com/dp/B010C78NQI

Thanks for your help!

* * *

ABOUT THE AUTHOR

Responding to God's call from the business world in 1992 to full-time vocational ministry, Ken Winter joined the staff of First Baptist Church of West Palm Beach, Florida, serving as the associate pastor of administration and global mission. In 2004, God led Ken, his wife and their two teenagers on a Genesis 12 journey, that resulted in his serving with the International Mission Board (IMB) of the Southern Baptist Convention. From 2006 until 2015, Ken served as the vice president of church and partner services of IMB, assisting churches across the US in mobilizing their members to make disciples of all peoples. Most recently, Ken served as the senior associate pastor of Grove Avenue Baptist Church in Richmond, Virginia. Today that Genesis 12 journey continues as Ken labors as a bond-servant of the Lord Jesus Christ in the proclamation of the gospel to the end that every person may be presented complete in Christ. The *Lessons Learned In The Wilderness* series is a collection of the lessons God has taught (and continues to teach) Ken and his family throughout their day-to-day journey with Him.

And we proclaim Him, admonishing every man and teaching every man with all wisdom, that we may present every man complete in Christ. And for this purpose also I labor, striving according to His power, which mightily works within me.
(Col 1:28-29 NASB)

* * *

OTHER BOOKS IN THE SERIES

The Wandering Years (Book #2)

Why did a journey that God ordained to take slightly longer than one year, end up taking forty years? Why, instead of enjoying the fruits of the land of milk and honey, did the Israelites end up wandering in the desert wilderness for forty years? Why did one generation follow God out of Egypt only to die there, leaving the next generation to follow Him into the Promised Land?

In the journeys through the wildernesses of my life, i can look back and see where God has turned me back from that land of promise to wander a while longer in the wilderness. God has given us the wilderness to prepare us for His land of promise, but if when we reach the border we are not ready, He will turn us back to wander.

If God is allowing you to continue to wander in the wilderness, it is because He has more to teach you about Himself – His Person, His purpose and His power. "**The Wandering Years**" chronicles through sixty-one "bite-sized" chapters those lessons He would teach us through the Israelites' time in the wilderness as recorded in the books of Numbers and Deuteronomy.

The book has been formatted for one chapter to be read each day for sixty-one days. Explore this second book in the "**Lessons Learned In The Wilderness**" series and allow God to use it to apply those same lessons to your daily journey with Him.

Possessing the Promise (Book #3)

The day had finally arrived for the Israelites to possess the land that God had promised. But just like He had taught them lessons throughout their journey in the wilderness, He had more to teach them, as they possessed the promise.

And so it is for us. Possessing the promise doesn't mean the faith adventure has come to a conclusion; rather, in many ways, it has only just begun. Possessing the promise will involve in some respects an even greater dependence upon God and the promise He has given you.

"Possessing the Promise" chronicles the stories, experiences and lessons we see recorded in the books of Joshua and Judges in sixty-one "bite-sized" chapters. The book has been formatted for one chapter to be read each day for sixty-one days.

Explore this third book in the **"Lessons Learned In The Wilderness"** series and allow God to use it to teach you how to possess the promise as He leads you in the journey with Him each day.

Walking With The Master (Book #4)

Our daily walk with the Master is never static – it entails moving and growing. Jesus was constantly on the move, carrying out the Father's work and His will. He was continuously surrendered and submitted to the will of the Father. And if we would walk with Him, we too must walk surrendered and submitted to the Father in our day-to-day lives.

Jesus extended His invitation to us to deny ourselves, take up our cross and follow Him. **"Walking With The Master"** chronicles, through "sixty-one" bite-sized chapters, those lessons the Master would teach us as we walk with Him each day, just as He taught the men and women who walked with Him throughout Galilee, Samaria and Judea as recorded in the Gospel accounts.

The book has been formatted for one chapter to be read each day for sixty-one days. Explore this fourth book in the **"Lessons Learned In The Wilderness"** series and allow the Master to use it to draw you closer to Himself as you walk with Him each day in the journey.

For more information about these books, including how you can purchase them, go to www.wildernesslessons.com

19615167R00108

Made in the USA
Middletown, DE
06 December 2018